Challenging Notions

Challenging Notions

Critical Victimology
in Canada

Tammy C. Landau

Canadian Scholars' Press Inc.
Toronto

Challenging Notions: Critical Victimology in Canada
Tammy Landau

First published in 2006 by
Canadian Scholars' Press Inc.
180 Bloor Street West, Suite 801
Toronto, Ontario
M5S 2V6

www.cspi.org

Canadian Scholars' Press Inc. gratefully acknowledges financial support for our publishing activities from the Government of Canada through the Book Publishing Industry Development Program (BPIDP).

Library and Archives Canada Cataloguing in Publication

Landau, Tammy
Challenging notions : critical victimology in Canada / Tammy C. Landau.

Includes bibliographical references.
ISBN 978-1-55130-308-6

1. Victims of crimes—Canada—Textbooks. I. Title.

HV6250.3.C3L36 2006   362.880971   C2006-906557-8

Cover design: Jill Miall
Interior design and layout: Brad Horning
Cover photo: Tammy Landau. Reprinted by permission of the author.

07   08   09   10   5   4   3   2

Printed and bound in Canada by Marquis Book Printing Inc.

Canadä

Acknowledgments

I LEARNED THE HARD WAY that writing a book is about more than scholarship, although that is at the core. It is also about ideas, opportunities and, perhaps most importantly, timing. The challenge is made enormously more bearable with a network of support during those times when putting words on a page seems impossible. I am grateful to have had many people in my life who provided me with the encouragement and kindness I needed to finish this manuscript.

Canadian Scholars' Press Inc. has shown enthusiasm for my work from the beginning. For their patience, and seeing me through the various hurdles of producing the final manuscript, I would like to thank my editor, Susan Silva Wayne, Martha Keenan, the production manager, and Jack Wayne, the publisher. Graphic designer Jillian Miall was wonderfully creative with the artwork for the cover and poster for the book. The research assistance of Holly Kerr and the administrative assistance of Annie Sperry were efficient and professional and made the transition from chapter to chapter much easier. I am grateful to Gail Kellough and Margaret Jackson for their valuable feedback on a previous version of the manuscript. Althea Prince provided guidance and encouragement in the early stages of the project.

Anyone who knows me just a little understands how much I value my family and friends. My parents, Frances and Al Lando, face the chaos of day-to-day family life with humour, dignity and a special warmth reserved for their children. My siblings, Barb, Bill, Gail, Howard and Cara, understand me and tolerate me like no one else can. While I have many special friends, a unique place is reserved for Ellen Cohen, whom I have kept very busy for the better part of our adult lives, and Sam Pelc (who can move from city to city but can never get very far away). Finally, Marcia Moshé has been a good colleague, a wonderful friend and a close ally since I joined Ryerson University some years ago.

I want to extend an especially heartfelt thanks to my students for engaging me, challenging me, teaching me and inspiring me to write this book. I hope they learn from my words even a fraction of what I have learned from theirs.

For Faye Anna-Pearl, Jacqueline Elise, and Johanna Esther.

Table of Contents

CHAPTER 1

Introduction to Victimology

THE SUMMER OF 1996 was a difficult one for Canadians. Paul Bernardo went on trial for the sex slaying of schoolgirls Leslie Mahaffy and Kristen French. The horrific details of the sexual abuse and torture they experienced before their deaths were meticulously recorded on video and entered into evidence at the trial. Visual documentation of the killings contained in the videos was considered too traumatic for the families of the victims to endure, and too degrading to the memories of the victims to be made public. While the jury was allowed to view the videos in their entirety, spectators in the courtroom, including the press, were permitted to hear only the audio portion of this evidence.

The Bernardo trial also revealed that the Crown prosecutor had entered into a plea agreement with Karla Homolka, Bernardo's wife, before the videos of the murders were discovered. In exchange for her testimony against him, Homolka received a 12-year sentence for manslaughter. Yet the videos, not released until Bernardo's trial, provided graphic evidence of her complicity in the crimes. Her claim that she was a "battered woman" and therefore less responsible enraged Canadians and fell on an unsympathetic and unresponsive public. There were calls to nullify the agreement, and to hold an investigation into the circumstances of the "deal with the devil."

Yet such a deal was not unprecedented. In 1982, Clifford Olson was convicted of the sex killings of 11 children in British Columbia. (See Box 1.1)

Box 1.1: Outcry Rages over $90,000 to Buy Killer's Confession

VANCOUVER—A public outcry against the "absolutely intolerable" payment of $90,000 to mass murderer Robert Clifford Olson mounted today within hours of the secret deal being made public.

MPs and lawyers—including Olson's defence counsel—protested the payment made "for the care of Mrs. Olson and her child" in exchange for the 42-year-old unemployed construction worker revealing where he had hidden the beaten and strangled bodies of seven of his 11 victims.

Olson, on trial for the murder of 10 of the children, dramatically changed his plea from not guilty to guilty on the third day of his trial yesterday. He was then charged with an 11th murder and again pleaded guilty.

Mr. Justice Harry McKay, sentencing him to life imprisonment, said parole could be considered only after 25 years. He added that he would recommend that Olson never be paroled.

British Columbia Attorney-General Allan Williams admitted in an interview yesterday that he had approved the payment of $100,000 to Mrs. Olson by the RCMP. Federal Solicitor-General Robert Kaplan said in Ottawa that he had known about the deal.

"However, the ethical dilemma of paying an accused murderer was outweighed by the horror of the crimes and terror gripping families in the province," Kaplan said.

Under the deal, Mrs. Olson was to receive $30,000 when her husband provided evidence to solve four murders and $10,000 per body when he led the police to seven of the victims' corpses.

Williams said $90,000 had been paid to Mrs. Olson but told reporters she would not receive the last $10,000 from the special fund set up by the RCMP.

Opposition politicians and lawyers—attacking the deal because it appears to make "murder profitable"—began calling for an immediate investigation.

Olson's own lawyer, Robert Shantz, called the payment "politically insane" and added that it was "morally wrong."

Toronto civil rights lawyer Clay Ruby said last night he was appalled. "There is a very real danger that people who would not kill may decide that $100,000 is enough to justify the need."

Pat McCann, a prominent Ottawa lawyer and former president of the Ottawa Defence Counsel Association, said: "It's almost like making crime pay—there's something really smelly about buying the conviction of a suspect."

Tory justice critic Allan Lawrence—the minister responsible for the RCMP—called for an investigation of the payments and said Kaplan cannot avoid responsibility. He could have stopped the deal even though he didn't know about it until two days after it was struck.

And NDP justice critic Svend Robinson, whose Burnaby riding is in the area where the murders were committed, said the idea that Olson's family could profit from the murders of children is "absolutely intolerable."

Robinson noted that evidence cannot be admitted in court if "there is any hope of a reward"—suggesting that the payment to Olson might have jeopardized a successful prosecution if he had not pleaded guilty.

Tory MP Walter Baker says he wants a full investigation by Justice Minister Jean Chrétien.

The incident might establish an ugly precedent that could, if followed by police, throw future convictions out of the window.

Kaplan insisted the unique arrangement is not a signal to criminals or potential criminals that $10,000 is available for every body they produce.

But lawyer McCann said that promise means nothing to some "warped character who wants to do something for his family. It seems to me it's a dangerous step."

Olson's lawyer said it was the first time in Canada that an accused had been paid money. "My opinion is (the Mounties) overstepped the moral bounds of investigation. I don't think the police should be paying a suspect accused of murder for information. I predict a full-scale inquiry will be held into the force's conduct."

While the psychopathic killer was beginning his 11 life sentences, Williams explained that the payments were made partly out of consideration for the parents whose children were still missing.

At first, Williams told reporters yesterday that he knew nothing about any money being paid to Olson.

But after special prosecutor John Hall confirmed the deal, Williams admitted it had happened and apologized for stonewalling.

Hall's public disclosure meant that the worst-kept secret of the case was made officially public.

Reporters knew about the deal soon after it was struck in August. And Williams himself had confided in newspaper publishers.

But nobody could write about it or broadcast it in case it wrecked the whole case against Olson.

Prosecutor Hall admitted the payments might have resulted in defence claims of "tainted evidence" but the case never got to that stage.

He said he agreed to the payments as "a matter of finding a solution to a very difficult case."

After Olson took police to the scenes, he admitted the killings, Hall said.

Shantz agreed that the police were under tremendous pressure to solve the series of brutal murders.

Source: *Toronto Star* (January 15, 1982), A1.

In that case, the Attorney General of the province paid Olson $90,000 in exchange for information about the whereabouts of the bodies of seven victims that had yet to be found.

According to reports at the time, the parents of the children wanted peace of mind, while the police were uncertain of obtaining a conviction with the evidence they had. The money went into a trust fund for Olson's wife and infant son and was considered "a bargain." "[T]he end result is that Olson goes to jail for the rest of his life and hundreds of thousands of people [in British Columbia] can go back to leading normal lives" (Cohn, 1982, p. A8).

Nor was this likely the first time that "deals" had been made with serious offenders in order to accommodate some of the interests of either the victims or the case for the prosecution. However, the extent of the involvement of the victims' families in the prosecution of Paul Bernardo was likely unprecedented. The families of Leslie Mahaffy and Kristen French were represented by independent legal counsel at every stage of the criminal process, and were permitted to make submissions to the court, which were independent from those of the Crown. At the same time, the parents of Tammy Homolka, Karla's 15-year-old sister who was also murdered by the couple, had no more involvement or consideration than the parents of an accused murderer.

In another high-profile case that summer, in another judicial forum, Madam Justice Louise Arbour conducted the Commission of Inquiry into Certain Events at the Prison for Women in Kingston, Ontario (Arbour, 1996). The Arbour Commission was struck after a video was released to the public showing inmates at the Prison for Women in Kingston being strip-searched by an all-male Institutional Emergency Response Team. The video, aired on television with the consent and permission of the women involved, showed the IERT entering their cells, ordering the women to take off their clothes or have them forcibly cut off, and removing the women from their cells. This was done to permit mostly male workers to conduct a "cell extraction," i.e., remove all items from the cells, including personal belongings, clothing, even the beds. The Correctional Service of Canada maintained that the response was necessary to restore order in the prison after a near riot by these same women, and the continued disruption inside the prison. Nevertheless, Canadians, along with the international community, were shocked at the women's treatment in the hands of correctional authorities.

After a year-long inquiry, Madam Justice Arbour found that the Correctional Service of Canada had violated many of the rules, regulations, and policies of the Correctional Service. (See Box 1.2)

Box 1.2: 2.3.4.3 What Occurred

In this case, the governing direction from the Warden in place from early April 23rd was that nothing was to be given to the inmates. The interpretation of this instruction varied somewhat depending upon who was on duty. In general, though, the regime was one of denial. Virtually none of the rights, privileges and conditions of confinement available in the general prison population or ordinarily available in segregation were provided.

Inmates were given bedding and meals, and from time to time some toothpaste, but not necessarily a toothbrush, toilet paper and, in some cases, soap, a towel, facecloth and pyjamas.

In addition to being denied their legal entitlements with respect to access to lawyers and exercise, they were denied telephone calls to others, including to the Correctional Investigator, books and activities, showers, cleaning, and the removal of garbage accumulation. As well, the segregation logs record frequent refusals of their requests for socks, clothing, ice, lights, pop and toilet paper.

They were denied visits from the Inmate Committee members, from members of the Peer Support Team (a group of specially trained inmates who support each other in times of crisis), and spiritual support.

On the evening of Sunday, April 24th, officers were directed not to speak to the inmates, and two days later they were directed not to do rounds.

That same evening, the water was shut off and remained off until Monday afternoon, when it was turned on and the inmates were advised that if there were any problems, it would be turned off again. The evidence indicated that the only reason for turning off water would be flooding, although there was no indication that flooding had occurred. Indeed, turning off the water appears to have aggravated the behaviour of the inmates and increased the throwing of urine.

In general terms, the reasons advanced for the denial of these rights and privileges were linked to the behaviour of the inmates. Not all these restrictions can be rationally attributed to security or safety concerns. They were more an attempt to reward good behaviour and punish bad. Even at that, much seems to have been governed by the discretion of individual staff members, and there was often no appropriate link between behaviour and denial. For example, after a period of disruption on the 24th, the inmates were reported to have quietened down. Thereafter, Correctional Supervisor Gillis ordered that five of the inmates were to get nothing and no one was to speak to them. The ostensible causal link between an improvement in behaviour and a further denial of rights and privileges was not one which Correctional Supervisor Gillis could explain. Nor is it clear that turning off the water following an episode of urine throwing should be expected to diminish, rather than increase, the potential for further throwing of urine, particularly since the toilets inside the cells could be centrally flushed from the outside.

It is particularly striking that the question of whether the denial of rights and privileges would escalate an already disruptive situation was never addressed. Indeed, during the course of this inquiry when this proposition was suggested to senior Correctional Service representatives, some appeared to express surprise and interest in the novelty of the suggestion.

Source: Madam Justice Arbour, *Commission of Inquiry into Certain Events at the Prison for Women in Kingston*. Report (Ottawa: Public Works and Government Services, 1996), 5.

While no criminal charges were laid in the case, the release of the report led to the resignation of the Commissioner of Corrections, and the implementation of numerous recommendations and reforms. This case raises a number of additional issues about victims and victimization: Were the women "victims"? Are they less deserving of our concern and consideration because they are offenders? Do we give sufficient attention to forms of victimization committed by the state and its institutions?

The scenarios recounted above highlight important issues with respect to how we understand victims and victimization. For example, what are the conditions under which we readily identify people or groups as "victims"? What is the most appropriate role of the victim in the criminal justice system? Are the due process rights of accused people at risk if we increase the role of the victim in the criminal justice system? Should we, or can we, limit our analysis to the arena of the criminal justice system? Do our definitions of "victim" readily accommodate systemic forms of victimization?

The emergence of the concerns of victims and victimization is a relatively new social phenomenon. This is also true within the study of criminology. While at least one early criminologist wrote about the characteristics of crime victims (Von Hentig, 1948), it was not until the 1960s and 1970s that a contemporary approach to victims of crime began to develop in both Canada and the United States. By the 1980s, Canada had a variety of programs for crime victims spread across the country, and the first federal victims policy (Rock, 1986; Young, 2001). In the years since, a powerful victims' rights lobby and a number of major victim-oriented initiatives have altered the landscape considerably at all levels of government, involving both the public and private sectors. The response has influenced both individual cases and the criminal justice response more generally. With the increased politicized nature of criminal justice policy, victims have become a powerful force in shaping the debates and our social, political, and legal response to them (Roach, 1999).

The study of victims has also emerged as a dynamic field within the academic world. This, too, has evolved slowly but surely over the last three decades, and has become firmly entrenched in theoretical approaches, which reflect critical feminist contributions to criminological theory and policy both inside and outside the criminal justice system. While a relatively new focus within criminology more generally, victimology raises many challenging intellectual and practical issues, such as the relationship between the victim and the state, the inherently moral dimensions of victim status, and the influence of various forms of social inequality on our understanding of, and response to, victimization.

Nevertheless, there is a noticeable shortage of texts on the study of crime victims in Canada. This text is designed to provide, in one scholarly source, an overview of the empirical, theoretical, and policy issues that have emerged from the study of victimology, and provide a critical foundation on which to evaluate them. It is intended to fill a gap for students and teachers that clearly situates the victim in the contemporary yet evolving world of criminology and Canadian criminal justice. The text has a particular emphasis on the relationship of crime victims to the social and political context in which victimization is defined, measured, and responded to.

THE (RE)-EMERGENCE OF THE VICTIM IN CRIMINAL JUSTICE AND CRIMINOLOGY

This book's approach to understanding victims, victimization, and victimology will focus on the emergence of the victim within the criminal justice system since the mid-1970s in Canada. While a major theme of this text is the "new" emphasis on victims of crime, it is perhaps most accurate to talk about the *re*-emergence of the victim in the criminal justice system. In fact, the victim historically played quite a significant role in the criminal courts. As McShane and Williams (1992) note, in pre-law societies, "victims and their relatives controlled the extent of retribution and, consequently, the extent of their satisfaction with the punishment meted out to the offender" (p. 260). Only during the Middle Ages did the state introduce systems of law in the name of the "King's peace" to reduce blood feuds (Young, 2001). The notion of "public harm" replaced harms against individual members of the community to protect against disruption to the social order.

According to Young (2001), "this conversion enabled the emerging state to take complete control over a conflict between accuser and accused, and resulted in the transformation of a compensatory award into a fine for the benefit of the royal coffers" (p. 6). The state came to replace the individual victim in criminal cases, and the victim's role became that of a witness in the state's case against the accused (Karmen, 2001). While a system of civil law developed to address the "private harms" of individual victimizations (Karmen, 2001), the victim in the criminal process became "the person whose primary function was to provide emotional credibility to the system of public prosecution" (Kennedy and Sacco, 1998, p. 50).

> [V]ictims lost the important right to determine the essence of a transgression and the state began to use law to define offenses independent of the victim's sense of harm. From the perspective of traditional victimology, this point marked the beginning of neglect of the victim. (McShane and Williams, 1992, p. 260)

Indeed, this secondary role of the victim has persisted, and, until recent times at least, could only be described as a weak cog in the wheels of justice. While the administration of justice relies quite heavily on victim co-operation to initiate the process, first by reporting criminal incidents to the police and later by acting as credible witnesses for the prosecution, they play a technical role often cleansed of its personal, emotional, and, at times, even its human dimensions. "Real harm has thus been subordinated to theoretical conceptions of *legal* harm and the definition of a victim becomes an artificial one" (McShane and Williams, 1992, p. 260, emphasis in original). Indeed, Christie (1997) has noted the irony of this transformation in the name of the public good:

First, parties are *represented*. Secondly, the one party that is represented by the state, namely the victim, is so thoroughly represented that she or he for most of the proceedings is pushed completely out of the arena, reduced to the triggerer-off of the whole thing. She or he is a sort of double loser; first, *vis-à-vis* the offender, but secondly and often in a more crippling manner by being denied rights to full participation in what might have been one of the more important ritual encounters in life. The victim has lost the case to the state. (p. 3, emphasis in original)

While the limited role of the victim in criminal proceedings has not changed significantly, there has been renewed interest in victims' rights, which began as part and parcel of a variety of social movements throughout North America in the 1960s and 1970s. Many groups who might otherwise have had conflicting interests converged to advocate for improved treatment of victims of crime. In particular, conservative politicians, feminist activists, and civil rights advocates were most effective in mobilizing the modern victims agenda, which has given it its complexity and texture in current debates.

For example, in the 1960s, reported crime rates in the United States had risen to an unprecedented level (Kennedy and Sacco, 1998), while the ability of the police and prosecutors to solve them remained low. Particularly problematic were the results of the first American crime victims survey, which found that large numbers of crimes remained unreported to the police (Kennedy and Sacco, 1998). There were two significant implications of these findings: Firstly, the police and prosecutors were losing ground in their fight against crime and, secondly, the agents of the criminal justice system would have to work harder to gain the support and trust of the victim, in particular in engaging with the formal criminal process by reporting incidents to the police. "[S]ome of the earliest victim programs were intended to facilitate criminal justice functioning rather than to ease victims' pain and suffering" (Kennedy and Sacco, 1998, p. 52). Thus we see the beginning of an alliance between the victim and the law and order interests of the state.

At the same time, debates about criminals having more rights than victims of crime emerged (Karmen, 2001). According to Fattah (1992a), "it could hardly have been a coincidence that the 'rediscovery of crime victims' happened exactly at the time when those of the new political right were in the process of implementing their law and order agenda and their punitive criminal justice policy" (p. 11). Fattah also points to developments that occurred simultaneously with the rediscovery of the crime victim, including a return to the death penalty (in the United States); the rise of neoclassical penal philosophy (i.e., retribution); a return to fixed, determinate sentencing; greater use of incarceration; denunciation of rehabilitation; emergence of incapacitation as a major objective of penal sanctions; and the emergence of the fear of crime as a major social issue.

The most vocal, persistent, and perhaps most successful advocates of the plight of the victim came from within the increasingly activist women's movement. Their agenda focused largely, although not exclusively, on two main issues: uncovering the nature and extent of violence against women, and addressing the criminal justice system's negative treatment of women who were victims of sexual offences. It became increasingly clear that a male-dominated criminal justice system exacerbated women's experiences of victimization. For example, women were treated as though they somehow contributed to their victimization through their dress, behaviour, or sexual promiscuity (Belknap, 2001). The male-dominated criminal justice system was identified as a significant source of the revictimization of women and girls, failing to respond seriously to their experiences or to represent their interests throughout the process (Karmen, 2001). "Girls and women victimized by boys and men cannot count on the men at the helm of the criminal justice system to appreciate the seriousness of the problem and to effectively protect or assist them" (Karmen, 2001, p. 5).

The civil rights movement had somewhat different, but equally significant challenges for the administration of justice. In particular, systemic discrimination by the criminal justice system against black victims and the accused were the focal point. For example, civil rights activists highlighted the harsh treatment of black offenders when the victim was white, but the weak response in cases of a white offender and a black victim, as well as the disproportionate number of black men in prison and on death row in the United States (Karmen, 2001).

In some ways, both the agenda of the women's movement and the civil rights movement fit in well with conservative politics of law and order, which saw the increased protections of due process rights of the accused as a direct assault on the war on crime (Roach, 1999). Garnering the support of two powerful and vocal groups for increasing support for victims fit nicely into this strategy.

THE CANADIAN CONTEXT

While there are certainly parallels between Canada and the United States, the Canadian context provided its own fertile ground for the emergence of a renewed emphasis on the victim in the criminal justice system. Indeed, it did not begin with either the Paul Bernard/Karla Homolka case or even the Clifford Olson deal.

Rock (1986) provides the most comprehensive description of the development of a federal victims policy in Canada, which he describes as "a number of different histories which were scattered across the face of Canada and deeply embedded in their own local contexts" (p. 263). He notes that before the 1980s in Canada, there were a few victim programs, such as rape crisis centres and transition houses. In addition, in the early 1980s, the federal Ministry of the Solicitor General supported a small number of programs geared toward victims of robbery to recover the property and to keep the victim informed of the case.

However, there were a number of pivotal events that gave impetus to the emerging response to victims' needs, many of which emerged largely from federal initiatives. For example, the Peace and Security Package of 1976 set the stage for more law and order criminal justice policies. While the Act abolished capital punishment in Canada, it simultaneously made provisions for a number of public security measures, such as long mandatory minimum sentences for murder, and a tighter system of parole. Ismaili (1997) similarly notes the political and politicized nature of the debate as it played out in the early days of the pro-victim/anti-abolition movement, which had little direct input from victims themselves.

Another significant development in advancing the victim movement was the Canadian Urban Victimization Survey of the early 1980s, conducted by the federal Solicitor General in seven communities across Canada. The survey had as its stated goals "efforts to meet the rights and needs of the victims of crime." While victimization surveys are fairly standard today, this early survey was an important step in piecing together a picture of victimization in Canada. The data would be accessible "to a wide variety of audiences concerned with the provision of services to victims, with effective policing, and more broadly, with the control and prevention of crime" (Solicitor General, Canada, 1983, p. 1). The results were released as a series of "bulletins" identifying for the first time the nature and extent of unreported criminal victimization, reasons for non-reporting, and fear of crime in these centres across the country (Solicitor General, Canada, 1983). The main focus thus remained with the priorities of the policing and law enforcement communities over more direct needs of crime victims.

According to Roach (1999), the rights revolution in the United States in the 1960s, which emerged in Canada with the adoption of the *Charter of Rights and Freedoms* in 1982, has most shaped the current political context of the victims' rights movement in Canada. He notes that the due process protections for accused people enshrined in the *Charter of Rights and Freedoms* often exceed the legal rights afforded to Americans through *Miranda* and other legal mechanisms. However, Roach notes that

> [d]ue process issues generally did not engage women, Aboriginal people, or racial and other minorities. The debates also did not include victims' advocates, who were only beginning to be recognized and cultivated by the government. The lack of input from these groups set the stage for future confrontations in courts and legislatures between the due-process rights of the accused and the rights of crime victims. (1999, p. 49)

In Roach's (1999) analysis, there are two trends in particular that have had a significant impact on the place of victims in the political arena. Firstly, "criminal justice could no longer be defined as a matter between the accused and the state" (p. 4). The Bernardo trial is clear evidence of this, with the legal representation of the victims' families at every stage of the trial. The interests of the victims' families were clearly seen to be, at least for some purposes, different from the interests of the Crown in the prosecution of the accused. Secondly, Roach refers to the "criminalization of politics [which] began when legislatures, courts, and the media focussed on criminal justice issues that were symptoms of social, economic, political, and cultural problems" (p. 4). For example, the death of Kimberly Rogers while under house arrest for welfare fraud raised questions about the trend toward the criminalization of poverty, which began in earnest in Ontario under Mike Harris's Conservative government in the 1990s. (See Box 1.3)

Box 1.3: Justice System Not Designed to Handle Welfare Fraud Cases by Keith Lacey

An expert in poverty law and Employment Insurance (EI) told a coroner's jury, people who commit welfare fraud should not be dealt with under Canada's criminal justice system.

"The criminal justice system is not the place to deal with people who are vulnerable," said Bruce Porter, who has interviewed thousands of welfare recipients in his career.

"The system is not designed for this."

Many judges don't feel welfare fraud should be dealt with under the criminal code either, said Porter.

These same judges, however, are forced under the current criminal justice system to adhere to criminal code statutes and have no choice but to mete out punishment as prescribed by statute, he said.

Statistics clearly indicate the incidence of welfare fraud over $5,000 is rare compared to the 450,000 or so people who collect social assistance in Ontario, said Porter.

Statistics he provided show an average of about 500 cases of welfare fraud per year in Ontario over the last several years.

The Employment Insurance Commission in Ontario in 2000 investigated almost 970,000 overpayments and issued 80,000 penalties without a single criminal prosecution, said Porter.

Rogers was sentenced April 25, 2001 to six months of house arrest, 18 months' probation and ordered to pay restitution after pleading guilty to collecting $13,500 in welfare benefits while collecting $32,000 in student loans between 1996 and 1999.

Rogers, who was pregnant, died from an overdose of anti-depressants. Her badly decomposed body was found in the sweltering heat of her West End apartment Aug. 9, 2001.

The inquest has heard that after Rogers was convicted of welfare fraud, her benefits were automatically suspended for three months. However, a successful court challenge resulted in her benefits being reinstated at the end of May.

All EI fraud cases handled by investigators are dealt with administratively with fines and repayments almost always the punishment, said Porter.

This is the only fair way to punish welfare fraud, he said.

The incidence of welfare fraud is dramatically lower than EI fraud, yet those convicted of welfare fraud are stigmatized, ostracized and often severely punished as criminals, he said.

Under the EI system, administrators are allowed to take into consideration the effects of punishment on the accused and their dependants and the circumstances of why the accused provided false information, said Porter.

In many cases he knows of, penalties and fines are waived if the effects of the penalty would devastate the person or dependants, he said.

The inquest is expected to hear from its final witness today.

Closing submissions are scheduled for next Monday and Tuesday before the jury begins two or three weeks of deliberations.

Source: Keith Lacey, "Justice System Not Designed to Handle Welfare Fraud Cases," *Northern Life* (December 4, 2002).

Rather than dealing with this case and others like it through changes to the living situation of women and men in poverty, these cases too often wind up in the criminal courts, which are equipped to do little more than punish.

> In an age of fiscal restraint and scepticism about social-welfare reforms, however, many demands for state activism are channelled into the criminal process. The punitive model can thus promote a criminalization of politics in which social, economic, cultural and political problems are primarily addressed through the use of criminal sanction. (Roach, 1999, p. 32)

This text presents and integrates victim issues from a critical perspective. That is, critical approaches, outlined in greater detail in Chapter 2, take into consideration the intersection of race, class, and gender and other forms of social inequality and constitute the lens through which victim-related issues will be considered. Importantly, the role of the victim in the criminal justice system and the inadequacy of relying heavily on the criminal justice system to address victims' needs will be threads throughout the chapters.

QUESTIONS FOR FURTHER CONSIDERATION

1. Consider the case of the Arbour Commission, discussed earlier. What are some of the factors that influence whether the women who were strip-searched are considered "true" victims?
2. In the struggle for victims' rights, what do you think that conservative, feminist, and civil rights groups had in common? What were common concerns? Which policies might the three groups support? Which might they disagree on?
3. Do you think victims should have independent representation at the trial of accused people? What are some of the reasons for and against such a policy?

CHAPTER 2

Challenging Notions:
The Social Context
of Victimhood

AS HIGHLIGHTED in the introductory chapter, attempting to understand who or what constitutes a "victim" poses significant challenges. Like the law, defining victims and victimizations is perhaps better understood as historically situated, continually evolving, often contested, and ultimately elusive. Our notions of the "victim" reflect the structural locations of race, class, gender, sexuality, and other social characteristics of the victim, and are infused with broader social values, moral judgments, and power relations.

It is not difficult to point to examples that highlight the elusive nature of "the victim." As the editorial in Box 2.1 suggests, the death of a police officer often evokes more outrage than the death of other equally law-abiding and "innocent" victims in our communities.

What is it about the role, status, and activities of officers that, for many, assign greater value to their lives than to the lives of others who carry out their jobs with an equal degree of commitment and integrity? In fact, women are at much greater risk of being killed in their homes by their male spouses than police officers are of being killed while on duty. Have the sheer numbers of women killed by their spouses blinded us to the tragic fact that many women live in constant danger just by virtue of having a male partner? Are they not often heroes for risking their lives to protect their children? Why do we tend to blame the victim for not simply leaving, but do not ask why police officers don't find safer jobs?

Box 2.1: Two Horrible Stabbings, Two Different Reactions
by Jim Coyle

By now, most people must feel as if they knew William Hancox. So familiar have we become with the details of his too-short life, it's probably not even necessary to identify him. We've seen his wedding pictures, his stricken parents and boyhood friends. We know the schools he attended, the sports he played. Most of all, we know that there is a wife and daughter he leaves and an unborn child he will never know.

It is in no way to demean the honorable life and appalling death of Detective Constable Billy Hancox to ask if many among us could say as much about Jennifer Copithorn.

He was 32. She was 24. He was a police officer. She was a bank teller. He was doing his job in Toronto. She was on the way to hers in Bowmanville. And on Tuesday last, within hours, each was stabbed to death.

To be sure, it never fails to shock when a cop is killed. To the community, it is profoundly upsetting. To the families, who must live with the constant low-grade fear that this might one day happen, it's surely pain beyond knowing. A cop's death is everything awful everyone says it is.

But on another level, it's not surprising that such things happen. It's to be expected, given the nature of the job, that police officers will occasionally come to harm. What's heartening is how seldom they do, the reality being that other more pedestrian lines of work produce higher fatality rates.

Still, judging by the coverage and reaction, we are so much more outraged at one of these murders than the other—at the slaying of a policeman who seems merely to have been in the wrong place at the wrong time than we are at the killing of a woman under circumstances all too familiar.

Ambushed and savagely stabbed. A former boyfriend charged with murder. A person, moreover, who police say was known to them and who has a violent history.

When a cop dies, we recall every officer who has fallen before. When a woman is hunted down, we rarely do, even though the list would be longer, the circumstances more bloody. For her, there are a few paragraphs, maybe a mugshot. Nothing of the same wrenching community horror.

If it says good things about our society that Billy Hancox is so mourned, his brief life so celebrated, there's a more sobering message in the fact Jennifer Copithorn's murder, by comparison, was met largely with a shrug. And why is that? Well, because that sort of thing happens all the time, doesn't it?

Hancox knew the risk, nine years ago, when he put on a badge. Copithorn surely didn't when she got involved. Maybe the reaction is so disproportionate to those truths because, in times of grief, we seek the easier path.

In the officer's killing, we draw, as we habitually do, the most simplistic of caricatures, white hats versus black hats, Beaver Cleaver with a badge against nothing less than evil. It gives us comfort.

In the killing of the woman, there are no such trite clichés to grab at. To look upon it is to acknowledge again society's failure to protect. It is less upsetting simply to avert the gaze.

As this bloody week ends, and two families grieve, we know more than we ever expected to know about Billy Hancox. We know little still about Jennifer Copithorn, other than that she was considered friendly by customers and that she chose at one time in her life to live with, and once must have loved, a man now accused of killing her.

And we also know, or should, that the next person found dying in a pool of blood is more likely to be an estranged wife than a cop.

Source: Jim Coyle, "Two Horrible Stabbings, Two Different Reactions," *Toronto Star* (August 8, 1998), A4.

There are many influences on our notions of victimhood. As will be seen from the following discussion, organizational constraints on media reporting influence our conceptions of the victim. At the same time, these images are deeply embedded in the broader moral, legal, social, and cultural influences of gender, class, and race. Scholarly attempts to understand victim status have not been successful in clarifying what it means to be a "victim"; however, critical scholars have identified social and political processes that both shape and limit our notions of victimhood.

MEDIA REPRESENTATIONS OF CRIME VICTIMS

One of the most important points to keep in mind at the beginning of our discussion on media representations of crime victims is that a main priority of media outlets (newspapers, television, radio) is to present "factual" information in an engaging and entertaining format. As Kennedy and Sacco (1998) point out, the distinction between news and entertainment is not always easy to make and may be more accurately described as "infotainment." In this broader context of infotainment, the newsworthiness of events is determined by a number of factors that have little, if anything, to do with the actual importance of the event.

> Contrary to the claims, conventions and culture of television journalism, the news is not a neutral product. For television news is a cultural artifact; it is a sequence of socially manufactured messages, which carry many of the culturally dominant assumptions of our society. (Glasgow University Media Group, 1976, cited in Viano, 1992, p. 29)

For example, crime news constitutes the fourth largest category of stories for newspapers and television after sports, general interest, and business. This is clearly an overrepresentation of the "actual" amount of crime occurring. In an analysis of the studies on media representation of crime news, Kennedy and Sacco (1998) found a number of trends. Not surprisingly, they found that crime news focuses on reports of violence, particularly homicide. "Several studies have shown that even though homicide is the *least* frequently occurring kind of crime, it is the kind of crime *most* likely to be reported in the newspaper or on television" (p. 27, emphasis in original). In addition, news accounts of crime focus on "common" or "street" crimes, such as homicide, robberies, or theft. Crimes of the powerful, including crimes committed by the state, are less likely to be reported. Finally, the amount of crime news reported is not reflective of the amount of crime in society as measured by crime statistics.

The content of crime news is rarely shaped by the dogged determination of the lone journalist pounding the beat. In the contemporary context, the police are the source of almost all crime news and essentially provide journalists with most of the key information about criminal events (Kennedy and Sacco, 1998). There are few alternative sources that can be accessed as efficiently, as quickly, and as routinely as the police (Chibnall, 1977; Ericson, 1989). This suits many of the organizational needs of media outlets: not only are the police as an organization the main repository of a large amount of information about crime, police spokespeople are credible sources as "experts" on the issue. This increases their value to news organizations in general, as well as to individual journalists on the "crime beat." In fact, journalists who challenge the police view of things may jeopardize their access to crime news in future cases. For example, when the *Toronto Star* published a series of articles on racial profiling by the Toronto Police Service (Rankin et al., 2003), then Chief Julian Fantino barred *Toronto Star* reporters from future press conferences held at police headquarters. With their main source of crime and policing news cut off, a number of these reporters had to be reassigned to other portfolios.

The focus of police work on criminals, as opposed to victims, further influences the nature of the details released to the public through the media. This often results in incomplete, inaccurate, or poor information available about victims of crime. Viano (1992) describes the process as "describing victims selectively and negatively, utilizing stereotypes that lead to blaming the victim while overlooking other, positive attributes of the victim; or by presuming to know what a victim thinks or feels" (p. 26). While victims may be able to provide the press with the emotional or alternative angle to a news story that is not provided by the police, they may not be good news sources for a number of reasons (Kennedy and Sacco, 1998). For example, victims may be difficult to access or even to locate. They may not be articulate or have personal credibility with the public. In some cases, they may have (or be perceived to have) their own agenda. From the perspective of victims, however, reporters are often insensitive to their needs, and may harass them or invade their privacy. In a heartfelt editorial to the *Toronto Star*, freelance journalist Miriam Porter and Avrum Rosensweig, a relative of David Rosensweig, who was murdered in Toronto in July 2002, recounted the lengths to which the media went in order to "cover" the grieving family in the days after the murder:

> Chavi Rosensweig, the widow of the deceased, and her six children, one of whom was only 11 years old, were forced to run to their cars to avoid the photos they did not want to appear in. The look of fear on the Rosensweigs' faces did not stop the photojournalists from chasing them, like paparazzi, as if they were celebrities.... We saw a number of photojournalists nearly push Chavi into the snow in order to secure a photo. Pictures of Chavi's children—their faces reflecting the depth of human suffering—were consistently seen in the media without permission from the family. Does the public benefit from seeing children the day after their father was stabbed to death other than for reasons of base curiosity? (Porter and Rosensweig, 2005, p. A19)

Clearly, the media and police organizations do not operate in a social vacuum. Rather, images of victimhood are a product of a variety of processes that reflect the social location of individuals and groups in society. As discussed below, mainstream approaches describe how individuals are ascribed victim status in the context of the relationship between the victim and the criminal justice system. A consideration of a more critical analysis of the underlying processes that contribute to this status will follow.

What Is "Victimology"?

Victimology is, in effect, a sub-discipline of criminology, the only discipline even remotely attentive to victims.... Like criminology, it is an empirically-driven science, a *rendez-vous* science defined by its attention to all things associated with victims, rather than a science unified by a common theory, practice, profession or institution. Like criminology, it may be described as diffuse, synthetic and loosely-integrated. (Rock, 1994, p. xvi)

As a close reading of Rock's words suggests, defining the parameters of victimology is not easy, nor is it necessary. By definition, it has a substantive focus on victims. However, like the study of criminology itself, there may be few common assumptions, theories, or overlapping themes that unite those who claim to "do victimology." While this text does not focus primarily on victimological theories, the foundations for the conceptual, practical, and policy work that defines much of the discipline cannot be overlooked. Attempting to slot fairly complex frameworks into a small number of categories is often risky; however, there are two broad frameworks into which most approaches to victimology can be placed. We will refer to these as *mainstream* approaches and *critical* approaches, both of which are briefly outlined below.

Mainstream Approaches to Victimology

Mainstream approaches to victimology focus on the victim and his or her relationship with the state, in particular within the institutional components of the criminal justice system. These approaches have been characterized as fitting within the assumptions of positivism, or what Walklate (2001) refers to as "conventional victimology" (p. 39). That is, they are based on consensus theories of criminal justice. How "victim" is constituted is generally considered to be unproblematic, as are ways in which victimization itself is classed, raced, gendered, and reflective of a range of social inequities.

In this vein, Meadows (1998) defines victimology as "the study of crime victims and their relationship to offenders and the criminal justice system" (p. 2). While early victimologists focused on identifying characteristics of victims and interpersonal relationships that increased the likelihood of victimization (Meirs, 1989; Von Hentig, 1948), the contemporary focus from this perspective is placed on the lack of consideration of the victim and victim-related issues within the criminal justice system. Meirs (1989) sums it up as follows:

> [P]ositivist criminology has traditionally concentrated on two aspects of victimization: the identification of characteristics inhering in individuals that make them especially susceptible to victimization, and the identification of particular crimes and of relationships between victims and offenders which might suggest some causal responsibility in victims for their victimization. (p. 3)

Some who work from within mainstream approaches have moved beyond the focus on victims *versus* the state or other offenders. For example, the interactionist or social reaction perspective shifts the focus to a different set of questions that emphasize the *process* of defining victims and victimization. Thus, the question becomes

> under what circumstances can individuals or groups of individuals (including entire ethnic or nations groups), animals, plants or even values or ideals become victims? What are the social processes by which such groups are selected and identified as "victims," and why are they so labelled? (Meirs, 1989, p. 4)

Interactionists, too, failed to address essential questions about the fundamental forces that drive social reaction and remain largely uncontested.

CRITICAL APPROACHES TO VICTIMOLOGY

Unlike mainstream approaches, critical victimology questions the very processes of defining victimization, and the social, political, and structural foundations that shape it. Grounded as it is in criminological theory (see Vold, Bernard, and Snipes, 1998, for an in-depth treatment of criminological theories), the developments within critical victimology have moved increasingly toward the inclusion of the structural basis of power relations and their impact on both individuals and groups. Critical approaches thus go beyond enumerating the descriptive to include processes of power and authority.

One of the earliest examples from within this framework comes from Quinney (1970, 1972), who recognized the power relations that underlie social and political processes, such as the creation and application of criminal law. That is, only some people had the power to define who was a victim (and criminal) and who was not. Quinney's work opened the door for a greater consideration of the sources and impact of power relations, and paved the way for approaches that have as their foundation the structural inequalities in the social world. Walklate (1990) highlights the critical dimension: "How is it that the [victim] label itself is constructed and who acquires the legitimacy of the 'ideal victim'?" (Walklate, 1990, p. 27).

From within this perspective, Marxist or radical criminologists ground their work on the material basis of power and the structural basis for class relations. They reject the neutrality of the police, courts, and corrections, along with the belief that these agencies act to protect society and the "public interest."

> [T]he radical criminological perspective challenges the explicit or implicit mainstream concept of law as a positive force based upon consensus, which impartially protects innocent members of society from harmful acts by predatory wrongdoers. If law *ultimately* expresses the interests of the capitalist enterprise it then follows that a formal concept of victimization is linked to these interests. (Friedrichs, 1983, p. 288, emphasis in original)

McShane and Williams (1992) identify the areas that would be of greater interest to radical victimology: "the definition of victim; an understanding of the victim's assigned role in our criminal justice system; and the use and abuse of victims by the politico-economic system, the criminal justice system, politicians, and the media" (p. 259). One important focal point would be on the working-class nature of most criminals and victims, and the ways in which an emphasis on crime diverts attention away from the state's role in creating crime, criminals, and reproducing an unequal social order.

While Marxist-oriented approaches introduced the importance of a consideration of class into the victimology discourse, feminist approaches have made equally important contributions to the analysis of the issues. Just as early Marxists focused almost exclusively on class, early feminist analysis often focused only on the impact of social processes on women and girls to the exclusion of race and other forms of social inequality (Stanko, 1995; Walklate, 2001). The coming together of feminist and Marxist ideologies laid the groundwork for the integration of the structural basis of other forms of social inequality, such as race, ability, sexual orientation, and age. In addition, contemporary critical approaches create the conceptual space to consider systemic forms of victimization as well as victimization either supported by or perpetrated by the state (Stanko, 1994). As such, victimology cannot adhere to a narrow focus on victims in isolation from the social processes that contribute to it in various forms.

DEFINING THE "VICTIM"

As noted earlier, mainstream definitions of the victim are firmly rooted in both the formal relations of the criminal process and positivist assumptions about crime and how to study it. The criminal justice system and related agencies typically frame the relations between victim and offender. In addition, however, these definitions generally reflect positivist assumptions about crime and its causes. For example, as positivists assume there is an essential difference between criminals and non-criminals, there is an inherent assumption about the differences between victims and non-victims. "[I]f criminals could be identified in some way then so could victims" (Walklate, 2001, p. 28).

From this perspective, victims are defined as those who, while having experienced a victimization, also had particular characteristics (as did offenders) and who could be seen as distinct from those in the population who were not victims of crime. As Walklate (2001) notes, criminologists considered victims in terms of "determinism, differentiation and pathology."

These are reflected in the work of those early victimologists whose typologies focussed on either the personal characteristics of the victim ... or the contribution that their behaviour made to the commission of a crime.... Arguably, this way of thinking about the victim reflects an underpinning view that there is a normal person measured against whom the victim somehow falls short. (p. 28)

The emphasis on both the distinctiveness of victims from offenders, and the passive nature of victims as the recipients of harm is pervasive. "One gets little sense from within this strand of victimological work of how the state (including the law) actively contributes to the victims we see or do not see, or of the ways in which individuals may actively resist, campaign against, or survive the label 'victim'" (Walklate, 2000, p. 186).

In addition, mainstream approaches are silent on the role of the state in victimizing (Green, 1994).

Hundreds of thousands of people have been killed, physically assaulted, rendered homeless and hungry, raped, or emotionally abused by the actions and policies of governments and state officials. State sponsored genocide, ethnic cleansing, and imperialism are clearly not actions of the past, but current, compelling and deeply disturbing problems which require immediate and rigourous scholarly study. (Kauzlarich et al., 2001, p. 175)

For example, generations of Aboriginal peoples in Canada have been subject to the state's deliberate policies to colonize, assimilate, and eliminate Aboriginal societies and their historical, social, and cultural foundations (Royal Commission on Aboriginal Peoples, 1996). While Aboriginal peoples have been successful in many of their claims, only a small proportion of them would be processed through the criminal courts.

However, there are additional limitations for understanding victims from a mainstream perspective. As suggested earlier, the reliance on the criminal process as the frame of reference marginalizes the victim to the role of witness for the prosecution. The process itself prioritizes the actions of the offender, and the state's primary interest in crime control, at the expense of responding to victims. Indeed, once the case has been resolved, the victim/witness ceases to exist in a very technical sense: the criminal process is not designed to provide any additional services to victims, or meet any additional needs they have outside the courtroom.

These limitations of mainstream approaches are significant. Critical scholars have expanded their conceptions of who or what constitutes a victim. Indeed, Quinney (1972) asserts that who is a victim is "optional, discretionary, and by no means innately given" (p. 314). Inevitably, the moral dimensions of victim status seep into the analyses.

> Taken together, for example, one could say that the way we selectively define, measure, and convey conceptions of victimization suggests that crime victims represent victims officially recognized as legitimate through a highly political process. Victims who challenge society's tenets, mores, and stereotypes are excluded from consideration, sympathy, and support or are included or grudgingly after a prolonged struggle for recognition. Those who suffer victimization by the state generally receive no recognition at all. (Viano, 1992, p. 29)

Indeed, there have been a number of attempts to describe the process of assigning victim status (e.g., Bayley, 1991; Christie, 1986). Christie (1986) explicitly integrates the victim, offender, and the broader power relations at play in defining the victim. He presents the attributes of the "ideal" victim—that is, a person to whom society quite readily assigns "the complete and legitimate status of being a victim" (p. 17). Accordingly, the ideal victim has the following "attributes": (1) the victim is weak; (2) the victim was carrying out a respectable project; (3) she was where she could not possible be blamed for being; (4) the offender was bad; (5) the offender was unknown and in no personal relationship to her; (6) the victim is powerful enough to make her case known and successfully claim the status of an ideal victim. According to Christie, the victim must be "strong enough to be listened to, or dare to talk. But she (he) must at the very same time be *weak enough not to become a threat to other important interests*" (p. 21, emphasis in original).

Fattah (1991) argues that some individuals who experience victimization are seen as "worthless" victims (p. 101) for a variety of reasons. "Inferior social status frequently is the deciding factor in determining who is a 'legitimate' victim. Therefore, lower-class individuals, racial minorities, and women are often held to be more 'legitimate' and deserving when they are victimized" (Weis and Borges, 1973, p. 78). Thus, social outcasts, such as sex trade workers, drug dealers, and, in our social climate, the homeless, are seen as acceptable and available targets. Indeed, Fattah (1991) notes that cultures designate certain individuals or groups as appropriate, even "deserving" (p. 101) targets for victimization, citing the example of old rape laws that made wives culturally appropriate victims of rape. In the contemporary climate, one might argue that children are appropriate cultural targets for the use of violence (Landau, 2005). In fact, the Supreme Court of Canada has recently upheld section 43 of the *Criminal Code*, which permits the use of corporal punishment against children (*Canadian Foundation for Children, Youth, and the Law vs. The Attorney General in Right of Canada*, 2004 S.C.C. 4) even though much child abuse begins as disciplinary action by parents. While the Supreme Court of Canada placed restrictions on the use of the force, such violence directed against any other person except one's own child would be considered assault under Canadian law.

Razak (2000) suggests that we *expect* some people, Aboriginal women in particular, to be victims of extreme violence and therefore accept it almost casually when it happens. These victims rarely report their victimization and when they do, it is met with little social or criminal justice reaction (also see Comack and Balfour, 2004). Her point is tragically reinforced by the case of roughly 50 missing women from Vancouver's East Side. Most of these women were sex trader workers and/or homeless, and a disproportionate number were Aboriginal. While Robert William Pickton has been charged with the murders of 27 of these women whose DNA was found on his pig farm in Port Coquitlam, British Columbia, questions have been raised about the length of time it took to initiate a serious police investigation, in spite of indications from the women's families and other members of the Vancouver community that the women had disappeared under suspicious circumstances. Many believe that had the women been more "respectable" (i.e., white, middle-class, and conventional in their lifestyles), the police response may have been different.

GENDERING THE VICTIM: THE CASE OF SEXUAL ASSAULT

At this point, we might begin a more focused analysis of gender as it relates to our understanding of victimization. "Gender becomes a crucial lens"

(Stanko, 1995, p. 210) because men and women experience victimization differently in terms of the nature, extent, and social contexts of its occurrence. In addition, it will become clear that our social response to victims, both inside and outside the criminal process, is deeply gendered. While it is difficult, if not impossible, to isolate gender from other social processes and structured inequalities, we will focus on gender as perhaps the most critical frame for assigning cultural and social meanings to both victims and their experiences.

Approaching victimization this way, victims are not neutral, isolated individuals who are judged solely on the basis of their passive experiences at the hands of their victimizers. Rather, they are active individuals whose behaviour is framed by their gender, class, race, sexuality, and age. These, in turn, contribute to our response to them as both individuals and members of groups. Gender provides the lens through which we can consider both femininity and masculinity, the response to women victims and men victims, and the social definitions assigned to victims largely on that basis. It will become increasingly clear that in many ways, the study of victimization is an analysis of gender in the context of the social scripts, moral judgments, and social reactions as they play out in a range of institutions, primarily the criminal law and the criminal justice system. A brief overview of the evolution of Canada's response to victims of sexual assault is instructive as it demonstrates the gendered nature of the legal and social response to these victims. While we may have made significant changes in removing the gender bias from the content of the legislation, the deeply problematic and prejudicial nature of the social response to both male and female victims remains.

Historically, the most serious sexual offence in Canada, as in many other jurisdictions, was rape, defined clearly in the *Criminal Code* as:

1. sexual intercourse by a man,
2. with a woman who is not his wife,
3. without her consent or with her consent if it was obtained by threats of bodily harm, fraud, or personating her husband (see Tang, 1998, for a review of the reform of rape laws in Canada).

The challenges in responding to incidents of rape were, in part, embedded within the legal constraints of the definition. For example, the definition centred on penile penetration, excluding other forms of sexual coercion.

The definition was also highly gendered: only women could be raped, only men could be rapists, and wives were largely excluded from victimhood as their consent to sexual activity with their husbands, coerced or otherwise, was implied in the marital relationship.

The prejudicial definition of rape in the *Criminal Code* was further exacerbated by the negative ways in which rape victims were treated, particularly by the police and courts. Indeed, generally low reporting rates for sexual offences (Clark and Lewis, 1977) were aggravated by the negative treatment women received when they did report their rapes to the police. Perhaps the most prominent example of this is the case of *Jane Doe v. Board of Commissioners of Police for the Municipality of Metropolitan Toronto et al.* (39 O.R. (3d) 487). "Jane Doe," as the victim became known, was raped at knife point in her own bed by a man who entered her apartment through the balcony door in the middle of the night. After reporting her rape to the police, Jane Doe discovered that a serial rapist, known as "The Balcony Rapist," was on the loose in her neighbourhood. Jane Doe also discovered that the police had a very good idea of the specific buildings he would likely strike, that he would enter through the balcony on the lower floors, and that women with distinct physical characteristics were at high risk. However, they did not issue a warning to the women in the neighbourhood because they didn't want to scare off the rapist; rather, they wanted to catch him before he moved on to another jurisdiction. While this might, under other circumstances, sound like a reasonable strategy, Jane Doe sued the Metropolitan Toronto Police Force (as they were then called) for using the women in the community as "bait" to catch the rapist at the expense of warning and protecting potential victims. Jane Doe alleged that the police were negligent in their response to the rapes in the neighbourhood, which violated her *Charter* rights and the rights of the other victims to security of the person and equal protection before the law.

During the course of the lawsuit, police records, memos, notes, and internal files on investigations into other rapes were produced for the court, and provided clear documentary evidence on the negative ways in which victims of rape were viewed by police at the time. Negative stereotypes of rape victims pervaded the investigation. For example, rape victims were seen to lie about being raped to get attention or to hide their unfaithfulness to their boyfriends. They were assumed to be unreliable witnesses and prone to exaggeration. (See Box 2.2)

Box 2.2: Discrimination

The plaintiff's argument is not simply that she has been discriminated against, because she is a woman, by individual officers in the investigation of her specific complaint, but that systemic discrimination existed within the (Metropolitan Toronto Police Force, or MTPF) in 1986 which impacted adversely on all women and, specifically, those who were survivors of sexual assault who came into contact with the MTPF—a class of persons of which the plaintiff was one. She says, in effect, the sexist stereotypical views held by the MTPF informed the investigation of this serial rapist and caused that investigation to be conducted incompetently and in such a way that the plaintiff has been denied the equal protection and equal benefit of law guaranteed her by s.15(1) of the Charter.

The MTPF has since at least 1975 been aware of the problems it has in relation to the investigation of sexual assault. Among those problems:

- survivors of sexual assault are not treated sensitively;
- lack of effective training for officers engaged in the investigation of sexual assault including a lack of understanding of rape trauma syndrome and the needs of survivors;
- lack of co-ordination of sexual assault investigations;
- some officers not suited by personality/attitude to investigation of sexual assault;
- too many investigators coming into contact with victims;
- lack of experienced investigators investigating sexual assault;
- lack of supervision of those conducting sexual assault investigations.

The force has conceded in public documents as in internal documents at least since 1975, that it has difficulties in these areas, that it will take immediate stops to remedy these shortcomings—yet the problems continued through to 1987 and beyond.

It seemed in that period that the public and persons who had brought their concerns in these areas to the attention of police were being publicly assured the problems would be eliminated, yet within the force the status quo remained pretty much as it had always been.

Every police officer who testified agreed that sexual assault is a serious crime, second only to homicide. Yet, I cannot help but ask rhetorically—do they really believe that especially when one reviews their record in this area? It seems to me it was, as the plaintiff suggests, largely an effort in impression management rather than an indication of any genuine commitment for change.

Former Chief of Police, Jack Marks, said that he would not have stood for problems like those outlined above continuing in the homicide squad for example.

He said, assuming he were aware of the problems, that he would "root them out" and "correct" them—yet these problems were allowed to continue over at least the better part of two decades in relation to the investigation of sexual assaults. Although the MTPF say they took the crime of sexual assault seriously in 1985–86 I must conclude, on the evidence before me, that they did not.

The rape trauma syndrome was clearly not understood by too many officers who were charged with the responsibility of investigating sexual assaults—others, including even some who had taken the sexual assault investigators course, adhered to rape myths. Examples can clearly be seen in this investigation—for example, Sgt. Duggan's occurrence reports in relation to the B.K. investigation—clearly slanted toward disbelieving the victim," to quote Margo Pulford. It is obvious to anyone that Sgt. Duggan was strongly influenced by the fact that a bowl of potato chips on the bed where the rape occurred apparently remained undisturbed. He concluded there had been no struggle and hence no forced sexual intercourse. His denial in this regard is simply incredible in the face of his own written record. Other examples are set out above as quoted from Det. Sgt Boyd's report and her comment that these problems existed in every station in every division of the force.

The protocol established by the force, AP No. 22, as it was designated, for the investigation of sexual assault was often not followed and when it was not there is no evidence that any senior officer or supervisor followed up.

The problems continued because among adults, women are overwhelmingly the victims of sexual assault, they are and were disproportionately impacted by the resulting poor quality of investigation. The result is that women are discriminated against and their right to equal protection and benefit of the law is thereby compromised as the result.

In my view the conduct of this investigation and the failure to warn in particular, was motivated and informed by the adherence to rape myths as well as sexist stereotypical reasoning about rape, about women and about women who are raped. The plaintiff therefore has been discriminated against by reason of her gender and as the result the plaintiff's rights to equal protection and equal benefit of the law were compromised.

Source: Excerpt from *Jane Doe v. Board of Commissioners of Police for the Municipality of Metropolitan Toronto et al.*, 39 O.R. (3d) 487, p. 519.

Not surprisingly, rape cases had higher rates of being determined by the police as being "unfounded." And, in spite of the force's public pronouncements that rape was second only to homicide in terms of its seriousness, officer training was weak. Madam Justice Jean MacFarland found that the case provided evidence of individual police officers' inappropriate behaviour in addition to prejudicial institutional policies of the police.

> In my view the conduct of this investigation and the failure to warn in particular, was motivated and informed by the adherence to rape myths as well as sexist stereotypical reasoning about rape, about women and about women who are raped. The plaintiff therefore has been discriminated against by reason of her gender and as the result the plaintiff's rights to equal protection and equal benefit of the law were compromised. (*Jane Doe v. Board of Commissioners of Police for the Municipality of Metropolitan Toronto et al.*, 39 O.R. (3d) 487, p. 521)

Madam Justice MacFarland found in favour of Jane Doe, and awarded her roughly $220,000 in damages. The Metropolitan Toronto Police Force did not appeal the court's decision.

In 1984, Canada's rape law was repealed and replaced with three levels of sexual assault. (See Box 2.3)

First and foremost, the changes removed the emphasis on penile penetration as the defining feature of the act. In addition, the new provisions removed the gendered way in which rape was defined. That is, both men and women could be either the perpetrators or the victims under the new sexual assault legislation. It was equally important, however, that the definition, grounded as it is in the criminal definition of assault, shifted the focus away from the sexual aspect of the offence to one that emphasizes the violence inherent in sexual offences. As Justice MacFarland noted in the *Jane Doe* case,

> [s]exual violence is a form of violence; it is an act of power and control rather than a sexual act. It has to do with the perpetrator's desire to terrorize, to dominate, to control, to humiliate; it is an act of hostility and aggression. Rape has nothing to do with sex, everything to do with anger and power. (p. 490)

The last several decades in Canada have clearly seen important changes to both the discriminatory aspects of the criminal law and some of the policies that have supported them. However, significant challenges remain for both female and male victims, although they are of a fundamentally

Box 2.3: Assault

265.(1) A person commits an assault when
- (a) without the consent of another person, he applies force intentionally to that other person, directly or indirectly;
- (b) he attempts or threatens, by an act or a gesture, to apply force to another person, if he has, or causes that other person to believe on reasonable grounds that he has, present ability to effect his purpose; or
- (c) while openly wearing or carrying a weapon or an imitation thereof, he accosts or impedes another person or begs.

Application
- (2) This section applies to all forms of assault, including sexual assault, sexual assault with a weapon, threats to a third party or causing bodily harm and aggravated sexual assault.

Consent
- (3) For the purposes of this section, no consent is obtained where the complainant submits or does not resist by reason of

  - (a) the application of force to the complainant or to a person other than the complainant;
  - (b) threats or fear of the application of force to the complainant or to a person other than the complainant;
  - (c) fraud; or
  - (d) the exercise of authority.

Accused's belief as to consent
- (4) Where an accused alleges that he believed that the complainant consented to the conduct that is the subject-matter of the charge, a judge, if satisfied that there is sufficient evidence and that, if believed by the jury, the evidence would constitute a defence, shall instruct the jury, when reviewing all the evidence relating to the determination of the honesty of the accused's belief, to consider the presence or absence of reasonable grounds for that belief.

266. Every one who commits an assault is guilty of
- (a) an indictable offence and is liable to imprisonment for a term not exceeding five years; or
- (b) an offence punishable on summary conviction.

Assault with a weapon or causing bodily harm

267. Every one who, in committing an assault,
- (a) carries, uses or threatens to use a weapon or an imitation thereof, or

(b)   causes bodily harm to the complainant,

is guilty of an indictable offence and liable to imprisonment for a term not exceeding ten years or an offence punishable on summary conviction and liable to imprisonment for a term not exceeding eighteen months.

Aggravated assault

268. (1) Every one commits an aggravated assault who wounds, maims, disfigures or endangers the life of the complainant.

Punishment
(2) Every one who commits an aggravated assault is guilty of an indictable offence and liable to imprisonment for a term not exceeding fourteen years.

Sexual assault

271. (1) Every one who commits a sexual assault is guilty of
(a)   an indictable offence and is liable to imprisonment for a term not exceeding ten years; or
(b)   an offence punishable on summary conviction and liable to imprisonment for a term not exceeding eighteen months.

272. (1) Every person commits an offence who, in committing a sexual assault,
(a)   carries, uses or threatens to use a weapon or an imitation of a weapon;
(b)   threatens to cause bodily harm to a person other than the complainant;
(c)   causes bodily harm to the complainant; or
(d)   is a party to the offence with any other person.

Aggravated sexual assault

273. (1) Every one commits an aggravated sexual assault who, in committing a sexual assault, wounds, maims, disfigures or endangers the life of the complainant.
(2) Every person who commits an aggravated sexual assault is guilty of an indictable offence and liable
(a)   where a firearm is used in the commission of the offence, to imprisonment for life and to a minimum punishment of imprisonment for a term of four years; and
(b)   in a other case, to imprisonment for life.

Source: *Criminal Code of Canada*, R.S., 1985, CC–46.

different nature. For example, the killing of two teenage girls outside a dance club late one Saturday led some to troubling commentary issues about how the girls' behaviour may have contributed to their own deaths. (See Box 2.4)

Box 2.4: Slain Teens Don't Sound "Ordinary"

Your April 7 front-page headline, "Teen slaying victims just ordinary kids," is both ludicrous and inaccurate.

How can two 15-year-olds who don't go to school, don't appear to live with responsible adults and are out after 1 a.m. in potentially dangerous areas be described as "ordinary kids?"

Such a tragedy isn't ameliorated by your trying to whitewash the circumstances.

Even today, I think that ordinary 15-year-olds live at home, go to school and are expected to be in by a reasonable time, though no doubt rebelling against their stuffy parents.

These young lives seem to have been a wasteland already, their prospects for a worthwhile life of love and family and personal achievement exceedingly dim.

It's not easy to be parents of teenagers at any time—in fact, it's hard and exhausting work—but someone has to be accountable for them.

And no, it's not society. Society didn't bring these children into the world.

Source: Letters to the Editor, *Toronto Star* (April 11, 1998), E8.

Why were they out so late? Were they behaving as "normal" girls of their age should? Did they engage in activities, or associate with people who should have alerted them to the dangers of what they were getting into? Perhaps more importantly, however, is whether we would be asking these questions if the victims were young males. Are any of these issues relevant to acknowledging the tragic loss of two young lives?

Not surprisingly, then, we are still faced with the fact that sexual assaults in Canada have the highest rates of non-reporting of all victimizations (Gannon and Mihorean, 2005). In the 2004 General Social Survey, 66 percent of all criminal victimizations were not reported to the police. However, this was the case for 88 percent of sexual assaults. Regrettably, the inadequacies of the criminal justice response to victims of sexual assault have not been addressed as much as would be hoped. For example, a recent audit of the Toronto Police Service's response to sexual assaults suggests that there have been improvements to the police response to sexual assault victims since Jane Doe's case came before the courts. However, many of the same problems, such as training of officers and failure to follow established procedures and protocols, remain (Toronto Auditor General, 2004).

Throughout this discussion, we have seen the critical contribution of feminist scholarship and activism to the most significant social reforms in responding to victimization. However, the emphasis on women's victimization reflects the political and social agenda to challenge the structural inequality experienced by women in various social spheres. In replacing the overwhelming emphasis in criminology on men as offenders, there has not, to date, been as much critical scholarship on men as victims. "The first point to be made is that there have been relatively few studies of male victims of crime" (Newburn and Stanko, 1994, p. 159). Victimhood cannot be thoroughly explored without it. For example, while the sexual assault provisions in Canada are now gender neutral, there are few data on the nature and extent of sexual assault among men (Goodey, 1997; Newburn and Stanko, 1994; Stermac et al., 1996; Washington, 1999). As Goodey (1997) states, "[o]ne can readily understand the research focus on women in light of their heightened and pervasive experience of victimization and fear. However, to ignore the male experience is to deny an insight into male vulnerability and, correspondingly, excludes an innovative appraisal of men as 'aggressors'" (p. 414).

For example, women are inundated with warnings about protecting their personal safety in a variety of ways (not walking home alone after dark, checking the back seat of their car before getting in, taking self-defence courses). The imagery of the "good victim" is presumptively female. Equally importantly, however, we expect men to be immune to victimization, as it is culturally constructed as a form of vulnerability that is generally excluded from traditional notions of masculinity. While women and girls are constructed to be perpetually at risk of most types of physical victimization, we are unable to accommodate similar notions of victimhood for men. "What is never questioned in the literature on crime, victimization, and fear of crime is masculinity" (Stanko and Hobdell, 1993, p. 413).

There are important empirical findings that highlight the complexity of masculinity, femininity, and victimization. For example, as will be outlined in greater detail in Chapter 4, men do, in fact, experience high degrees of victimization, which, in some contexts, exceeds that of women (Gannon, 2005; also see Walklate, 2001). For example, while women are more likely to be sexually assaulted, men are at greater risk of non-sexual assault. Nevertheless, women continue to express more fear than do men in a variety of situations: when relying on public transit alone at night (58 percent vs. 29 percent), when home alone at night (27 percent vs. 12 percent), and walking alone after dark (16 percent vs. 6 percent) (Mihorean, 2005a). As Stanko rightly points out, "[t]ry as they might, women are unable to predict when a threatening or intimidating form of male behaviour will escalate to violence. As a result, women are continually on guard to the possibility of men's violence" (Stanko, 1985, p. 1). At the same time, however, there is the "untested assumption" (Stanko, 1994, p. 160) that men are unwilling to discuss their own feelings of insecurity, vulnerability, or fear, which accounts, to some extent, for the lack of empirical research on this topic. Indeed, Goodey (1997) found that 11-year-old boys not only expressed fear "when outside in public places" (p. 407), but expressed more fear than did girls at this age. The main source of their fear? Older boys.

While the emphasis on the victimization of women is situated in their structural vulnerability, male vulnerability must be equally located in sustaining male dominance, power, and control. "Although it is the case that not all men are violent ... violence and its avoidance pervades men's maturation from childhood through adolescence and not unusually into adulthood" (Stanko, 1995, p. 216). Nevertheless, we do not sufficiently problematize either men's aggression or victimization, as the former is assumed to be natural and the latter to be unlikely. Washington (1999) discusses the "second assault" of male victims who do seek help:

> Lack of services for male sexual assault survivors as well as silence, secrecy, and misinformation within helping professions regarding this topic all contribute to revictimizing male survivors who seek assistance in the aftermath of sexual violence. (p. 715)

As has been alluded to earlier in this chapter, gender does not operate alone or in a vacuum. Rather, it intersects with other social locators, in particular, race, class, age, and sexuality. In this context, Goodey (1997) discusses the "fearless façade" adopted by boys as they mature:

> At its extreme, "fearlessness" can be expressed as physical aggression among working-class boys in their attempt to assert their masculinity. In comparison, middle-class boys, while also having to take on the masculine criteria of fearlessness, are able to and tend to project their masculine hegemony through different channels, such as academic success, and, therefore, are able to avoid the arena of physical aggression to which working-class boys can be reduced. (p. 410)

In Canada, we might look to the high rates of victimization of Aboriginal peoples as both victims and offenders, presented in more detail in Chapter 6 (Brzozowski et al., 2006). In particular, Aboriginal boys and men in residential schools and, more contemporarily, in their own communities are at elevated risk (Jacobs, 1998) when compared to non-Aboriginal men and boys. The legacy of colonization, dislocation, and abuse has contributed to both their higher rates of crime and victimization. Focusing on the offending of Aboriginal men, as implied by the emphasis on their overrepresentation in the institutional side of the criminal justice system, overlooks the complex ways in which the structural location of individuals and groups contributes to their lives. Without a more in-depth and critical analysis of gender (both masculinity and femininity), race, class, and other social characteristics, we fall woefully short.

We turn now to the ways in which victimization is measured, both officially and unofficially. As will become evident, the limitations of mainstream definitions of "the victim" spill over into the ways in which we come to know about victims and victimization — through the methods we use to measure it and to how this information is disseminated and integrated into the social world. As Elias (1986) has noted,

> [W]hile some claim that we have not collected enough data, the more frequent (and truer) complaint suggests that our data far outstrip our theories. Our excessive empiricism without theoretical foundations has brought a flood of data with which we often can make little sense. (p. 22)

While no theoretical "answers" will be provided to explain patterns of victimization, the following chapter provides a framework for thinking about measurement and analysis of data on victimization.

QUESTIONS FOR FURTHER CONSIDERATION

1. Apply Christie's characteristics of the "ideal victim" to victims of sexual assault. What factors might make some individuals (both men and women) "good" versus "bad" victims?
2. What effects have the *Criminal Code* changes from "rape" to "sexual assault" had on our response to victims of sexual violence? Include a consideration of both male and female victims.
3. Compare and contrast a mainstream and a critical approach to:
    (a) gang violence
    (b) assaults on sex workers
    Which do you think is likely to lead to long-term solutions to the problem? Why?

CHAPTER 3

Measuring
Victimization

AS IN OTHER social sciences, victimology relies on a variety of methods to collect data on the nature and extent of victimization and related issues. The purposes of measuring victimization are varied and depend largely on who or which agency is collecting the data. We may want to establish the amount of victimization of various types, the risk factors for specific individuals or groups, the context in which various forms of victimizations occur, or the impact of victimization at a personal, social, or community level. As will become evident in the discussion below, the different tools we have of measuring victimization often reflect the institutional, organizational, or professional interests of those collecting the data. Their particular value will then depend on the specific uses to which the data will be put.

In recent decades, we have seen the integration of a variety of approaches to piece together the picture of victimization. While police-related statistics are the most heavily relied upon, there is increasingly a role for victim surveys and self-report studies. Due to the limitations of these traditional tools, more work needs to be done in measuring systemic forms of victimization, such as racism, or institutional and state-sponsored violence.

UNIFORM CRIME REPORTS

It should not be surprising that the measurement of victimization has traditionally taken a back seat to the measurement of criminals. This stems from both the marginal role that victims have historically been given in the social world, as well as the primary emphasis in the administration of justice to detect crime and prosecute criminals. Indeed, one of the most established, if limited, forms of measuring victimization has been restricted to the tools used by the police to count crime: Uniform Crime Reports. As will be seen, the Uniform Crime Reports (UCR) are designed for measuring crime as opposed to measuring victimization, and identifying offenders as opposed to identifying victims.

The Uniform Crime Reports, originally instituted in Canada in 1962, are based on data collected from police services across country. In each jurisdiction, standardized information is collected on all *Criminal Code* offences, except *Criminal Code* traffic offences. For any given "incident," only the most serious crime is recorded. The information produced by the UCR is based on those "occurrences," which are substantiated by the police and include the number of reported offences, the number of actual offences, the number of offences cleared by charge, the number of people charged by sex, and the age category (adult or youth) of those charged.

In its earliest form, the UCR did not collect information on victim characteristics. Police organizations have been far more interested in measuring crime and offenders rather than victims and victimizations. In this context, victims have been primarily responsible for initiating the crime-reporting process. They were critical witnesses to the police task of identifying and catching offenders; however, many details of their experiences remained incidental and outside interests of police.

More recently, revisions have been made to the existing Uniform Crime Reports and some police services now use the Incident-Based Uniform Crime Reports 2 (UCR2), which include information on all criminal incidents reported to the police (not just the most serious offence), the age and sex of the victim and the accused, the relationship between the victim and the accused, and the location of the incident (Wallace, 2003). (See Box 3.1)

Problems remain, however, even with the UCR2. For example, not all police services participate: in 2003, only 123 police services submitted data under the UCR2, representing 59 percent of the police services in Canada

Box 3.1

GENERAL OCCURRENCE

NAME AND ADDRESS OF INSURANCE CO. OR ADJUSTER NOTIFIED	WARRANT STAMP	UNIT ASSIGNED	SOLVABILITY
		OFFICER ASSIGNED (BADGE NO.)	
THEIR FILE NO.	DATE NOTIFIED		

TYPE OF OCCURRENCE

	DOMESTIC * ○ Y ○ N	PLACE OF OFFENCE		OCCUPANCY CODE	ZONE
REPEAT ○ Y ○ N	SPOUSAL * ○ Y ○ N				
CHILD ABUSE ○ Y ○ N	IF YES, ARE CHILDREN INVOLVED ? ○ Y ○ N	TYPE OF PREMISES		NEIGHBOURHOOD WATCH COMM. ☐	PATROL AREA
ELDER ABUSE ○ Y ○ N					

DATE AND TIME OF OFFENCE	DAY OF WEEK OR BETWEEN	DATE	TIME OR BETWEEN

VICTIM (SURNAME, G1 & G2) (IF FIRM, NAME AND TYPE OF BUSINESS)

	CHECKS NIGHT DIRECTORY ☐ CPIC ☐	SEX	DOB	OCCUPATION
		CONDITION OF VICTIM		

RELATIONSHIP OF ACCUSED/SUSPECT TO VICTIM	PRESENTLY LIVING TOGETHER *	ALCOHOL/ DRUG CONSUMPTION VICTIM *	VICTIM SERVICES CONTACTED ○ Y ○ N VICTIM REFUSED ○ Y ○ N
HOME ADDRESS		POSTAL CODE	TELEPHONE (RES.)
BUSINESS ADDRESS		POSTAL CODE	TELEPHONE (BUS.)

REPORTED BY (SURNAME, G1 & G2)

	VICTIM ○ WITNESS ○ OTHER ○ CPIC CHECKED ☐	SEX	DOB	OCCUPATION
		CONDITION OF PERSON REPORTING		

RELATIONSHIP TO VICTIM		
HOME ADDRESS	POSTAL CODE	TELEPHONE (RES.)
BUSINESS ADDRESS	POSTAL CODE	TELEPHONE (BUS.)

HOW ATTACKED (COMMITTED OR ENTRANCE GAINED)	MEANS OF ATTACK (WEAPONS - TOOLS USED)	MOST SERIOUS WEAPON AT SCENE OF CRIME *
OBJECT OF ATTACK (MOTIVE - TYPE OF PROPERTY STOLEN)	VICTIMS / SUSPECTS VEHICLE INVOLVED (YEAR, MAKE, TYPE, COLOUR, LICENCE NO.)	

SAFE ATTACKED YES ○ NO ○	ALARM SYSTEM INSTALLED YES ○ NO ○	ALARM ACTIVATED YES ○ NO ○	NAME OF ALARM COMPANY (IF MORE THAN ONE, NOTE ON A SUPPLEMENTARY REPORT)		
NO LOSS OF PROPERTY IN THIS OFFENCE ☐	PROPERTY RECOVERED ALL ○ PART ○ NONE ○	WAS PROPERTY INSURED YES ○ NO ○	TOTAL VALUE OF STOLEN PROPERTY $	TOTAL VALUE OF PROPERTY DAMAGED $	UNIT COMMANDER'S MORNING REPORT YES ○ NO ○
CAN SUSPECT(S) BE IDENTIFIED YES ○ NO ○	BY WHOM (SURNAME, G1)	APPOINTMENT TO VIEW PHOTOS YES ○ NO ○	WHEN	RESULTS / LOOK-A-LIKES	COMPLAINANT ADVISED NO FURTHER ACTION YES ☐

SUSPECT NO.1 (SURNAME, G1, G2, NICKNAMES)			SEX	AGE	HEIGHT	WEIGHT	HAIR	EYES
ADDRESS, CLOTHING AND ADDITIONAL DESCRIPTION OF SUSPECT NO. 1		COLOUR WHITE ○ BLACK ○ BROWN ○	MTP NO.		CPIC CHECKED BY	ON FILE ○ NOT ON FILE ○		
		DOB	ARRESTED YES ○ NO ○			CHECK IF MORE SUSPECTS ON ATTACHED SUPPLEMENTARY REPORT ☐		

FOR ITEMS MARKED YES BELOW INCLUDE RELEVANT INFORMATION ON A SUPPLEMENTARY REPORT	WARRANT ISSUED FOR - LIST SURNAMES ONLY (SURNAME, G1 & DESCRIPTIONS) ON A SUPPLEMENTARY REPORT		RETURN AREA
AREA CANVASSED YES ○ NO ○	INFO RECEIVED YES ○ NO ○	METRO ALERT YES ○ NO ○ ADVISE WHEN CULPRIT KNOWN BUT NO FURTHER ACTION TO BE TAKEN	
AREA SEARCHED YES ○ NO ○	PHYSICAL EVIDENCE AT SCENE YES ○ NO ○		
FIS CONTACTED YES ○ NO ○	ANALYST'S RECORDS CHECKED YES ○ NO ○	DATE & TIME COMPLAINT RECEIVED	DATE & TIME OF INITIAL INVESTIGATION
CSO CPO REQUIRED YES ○ NO ○	MAJORED YES ○ NO ○	REPORT PREPARED BY (SIGNATURE)	RANK BADGE PLATOON ESCORT'S BADGE NO. DATE TIME
SUPERVISOR NOTIFIED YES ○ NO ○	NOTIFIED ○ ATTENDED ○	CHECKED BY SUPERVISOR (SIGNATURE)	RANK BADGE PLATOON DATE TIME UNIT
DET. OFFICE NOTIFIED YES ○ NO ○	NOTIFIED ○ ATTENDED ○		

(Wallace, 2003). With the exception of the data from Quebec and Ontario, urban police departments are overrepresented in those participating.

There are, nevertheless, additional limitations that relate more to relying on police-reported crime than with the specific tool used to measure it. At the core, we find a highly discretionary process in which much information is filtered out along the way. In the final analysis, police-generated crime statistics reflect the nature of those decisions, not the amount of crime or victimization in the community. Lost is the "dark figure" of crime, which does not come to the attention of police or other criminal justice officials. Some of the most critical characteristics in that filtering process are identified below. They apply equally to both the UCR and UCR2.

Reporting to Police: What we know from police-generated statistics is based only on incidents that are reported to the police. This is highly problematic, since most of police work is reactive (Ericson and Baranek, 1982). That is, in detecting and responding to crime, the police generally rely on information from the public. The vast majority of victimizations are not reported to the police. The reporting rate varies, however, according to the nature of the offence: 60 percent of assaults and over half of all robberies were not reported to the police (Gannon and Mihorean, 2005). As noted in Chapter 2, sexual assaults had the highest non-reporting rates at 88 percent (Gannon and Mihorean, 2005).

Definition of "Crime": After police receive information about a reported crime, they make critical assessments about each incident. Specifically, they decide whether a report is "founded" or "unfounded." This roughly corresponds to assessments of whether the event or crime actually occurred. Only those cases adjudged by the police to have actually occurred end up in the Uniform Crime Reports. While there are clear legal factors that influence this decision such as the strength of the evidence, as we saw from the *Jane Doe* case, some decisions are embedded within social judgments about credibility and social worth. The experiences of many victims of sexual assault, discussed in Chapter 2, are instructive here.

Changes in Legislation: The Uniform Crime Reports are linked directly to definitions in the *Criminal Code*. However, the *Criminal Code* is constantly changing the ways in which specific offences are defined by broadening definitions, narrowing definitions, eliminating offences, or including new ones. The Uniform Crime Reports cannot easily reflect those changes. Broadening the definition of a particular crime may lead to an increase in the occurrences as documented by the police, but which may not necessarily reflect an increase in that activity in the community. For example, as noted in Chapter 2, the three levels of sexual assault that replaced rape laws in 1986 cover a much broader range of behaviours. One might expect more sexual offences to be counted once the new legislation came into effect. At the same time, however, it is difficult to make comparisons over time since the offences are not defined in the same way.

Changes in Policy and Practice: Police detection of most criminal activity is reactive. However, the detection of some crimes is the result of proactive police work, and depends less on public reporting. For example, prostitution, drug-related offences, and impaired driving (Wallace, 2003) are often the result of "undercover" police work, or targeted police enforcement practices where considerable police resources are directed toward detecting and prosecuting specific types of crimes. An example here would be "R.I.D.E." ("Reduce Impaired Driving Everywhere") programs, which run all year round but which are expanded by police services around holiday times. Policies such as these may lead to an increase in police-recorded crime, but do not likely reflect an increase in actual crime.

Linking Police Statistics with Police Effectiveness: A considerable problem with the creation of crime statistics, and their use as an indication of the amount of crime in the community, is that they are, at the same time, employed as a primary measure of police effectiveness. That is, the volume of crime, as measured by the UCR/UCR2, is used in a number of ways to indicate how much work the police are doing and how well they are doing it. The sheer volume of crime to which a police service must respond is often used at budget time to assess the allocation of police resources from year to year. Increases in crime statistics, either overall or with respect to certain categories of offences (such as weapons offences or property crimes), suggest that the police need more resources (officers, vehicles) to keep up with the job. However, police also rely heavily on "clearance rates" and decreases in crime as indications of their effectiveness. Increases also suggest, however, that police may not be as effective in preventing crime, and they may come under criticism. This complex dynamic may encourage the selective use of police statistics for political purposes, which have little to do with how much criminal activity or victimization is actually occurring.

It should not be concluded from the foregoing discussion that there are no benefits in relying on police-generated statistics. Indeed, they give us some indication of the community's priorities in reporting crime, and the nature of the police response to those events. But they are fairly limited in giving us reliable, sound data on the nature and amount of criminal victimization.

VICTIMIZATION SURVEYS

The development of alternative ways of measuring victimization can be linked to attempting to uncover the "dark figure" of crime, as well as to the emerging focus on victims within the criminal justice system (Besserer and Trainor, 2000). In the early 1980s, the Solicitor General of Canada acknowledged that crime statistics "are based on reported crimes, or on police interventions or on results of prosecutions, and are often contradictory. They are all deficient in providing a true insight into actual criminal activity in Canada" (Solicitor General, Canada, 1983, p. 1). Since then, victimization surveys have been used in Canada and elsewhere to supplement police reports on crime. These are surveys that, as their title suggests, are based on information from victims, "the people themselves" (Solicitor General, Canada, 1983, p. 1). Indeed, the first large-scale, govern-ment-sponsored victimization survey in Canada focused on "the risks and impact of victimization, the extent and distribution of reported and unreported crime in our communities, and ... public awareness of, and participation in, crime compensation and crime prevention programs" (Solicitor General, Canada, 1983, p. 1). With time, however, a much broader range of victim-related issues have been integrated into the survey.

In a nutshell, victimization surveys are any type of survey in which the victim is the main source of information about the victimization experience. There is no requirement that the victimization be reported to the police either before or after the survey. Ideally, the survey is administered to a representative sample of the group of interest, but that often depends on the specific goals of the researchers. For example, there may be interest in establishing overall rates of victimization in a particular community, in which case a representative sample of that community would be desirable. Others, however, might be more interested in the victimization experiences of women who are assaulted by their partners, or in elderly victims of abuse. In those cases, obtaining representative samples of that more focused population would be important.

There is no one way in which victimization surveys are conducted. The administration of the survey may be done over the telephone, in person, or through the electronic or traditional mail. Questions may be either structured or unstructured in nature; the main criterion would be that they focus on eliciting information *from the victim* about that experience. For example, questions might ask if the respondent had been the victim of an assault in the past year (or in the past five years, or ever), details about the incident, if the victim was injured, if the assailant was known to the victim, any relationship to the assailant, and if the assault was reported to the police or other social agencies. Great care must be taken to clearly define the various terms as *Criminal Code* definitions are highly complex and not expressed in language typically used in our day-to-day lives. As with most types of survey research, the identity of respondents typically remains anonymous and their responses confidential. (See Box 3.2)

There are clearly numerous advantages to victimization surveys over police-generated statistics for obtaining data on victimization. Given the wide range of ways in which victimization surveys may be conducted, it is critical to assess each instrument and each implementation on its own merits. However, some of the more common advantages of victimization surveys over police-reported data are identified below.

Greater Accuracy for Some Types of Offences: As indicated earlier, the extent to which criminal victimizations are reported to the police varies across offence types. Most sexual offences and many forms of family violence remain unreported. Victimization surveys, conducted sensitively, anonymously, and under appropriate conditions, may be more accurate in assessing the nature and extent of these crimes, which do not depend on reporting to any other agency.

More Accurate Picture of the Victimization Context: Because victimization surveys are specifically designed for this purpose, they may be more effective in painting a broader picture of the context of victimization, including characteristics of the victim, the circumstances surrounding the incident(s), the nature of the relationship between the victim and the assailant, and the impact of the experience on the victim. This may also include eliciting information on how victims responded to their experience, whether they reported the incident to the police or other criminal justice

Box 3.2: Criminal Victimization

Assault

Now I'm going to ask you about being attacked in the past 12 months. An attack can be anything from being hit, slapped, pushed or grabbed, to being shot or beaten. Remember that all information provided is strictly confidential. (Excluding incidents already mentioned, and excluding acts committed by current or previous spouses or common-law partners,) were you attacked by anyone in the past 12 months?

How many times did this happen?
(Excluding incidents already mentioned and again excluding acts committed by current or previous spouses or common-law partners), during the past 12 months, did anyone threaten to hit or attack you, or threaten you with a weapon?

How many times did this happen?
Excluding acts committed by current or previous spouses or common-law partners, during the past 12 months, did anyone threaten to hit or attack you, or threaten you with a weapon?
(Excluding incidents already mentioned), during the past 12 months, has anyone forced you or attempted to force you into any unwanted sexual activity, by threatening you, holding you down or hurting you in some way? This includes acts by family and non-family but excludes acts by current or previous spouses or common-law partners. Remember that all information provided is strictly confidential.

How many times did this happen?
(Apart from what you have told me), during the past 12 months, has anyone ever touched you against your will in any sexual way? By this I mean anything from unwanted touching or grabbing, to kissing or fondling. Again, please exclude acts by current or previous spouses or common-law partners.

How many times did this happen?
(Apart from what you have told me), were there any other crimes that happened to you during the past 12 months, which may or may not have been reported to the police? Again, please exclude acts by current or previous spouses or common-law partners.

What were these crimes?

How many times did this happen?

Abuse by Current Spouse/Partner

Now I would like to ask you about some things concerning your spouse/partner. We're interested in knowing how long you've been married or living together.

I'm going to read a list of statements that some people have used to describe their spouse/partner. I'd like you to tell me whether or not each statement describes your spouse/partner.

Please remember that all information provided is strictly confidential. He/She tries to limit your contact with family or friends. Does this statement describe your spouse/partner?

He/She puts you down or calls you names to make you feel bad. Does this statement describe your spouse/partner?

He/She is jealous and doesn't want you to talk to other men/women. Does this statement describe your spouse/partner?

He/She harms, or threatens to harm, someone close to you. Does this statement describe your spouse/partner?

He/She demands to know who you are with and where you are at all times. Does this statement describe your spouse/partner?

He/She damages or destroys your possessions or property. Does this statement describe your spouse/partner?

He/She prevents you from knowing about or having access to the family income, even if you ask. Does this statement describe your spouse/partner?

Physical and Sexual Violence by Spouse/Partner

It is important to hear from people themselves if we are to understand the serious problem of violence in the home. I'm going to ask you ten short questions and I'd like you to tell me whether, in the past 5 years, your current spouse/partner has done any of the following to you. Your responses are important whether or not you have had any of these experiences. Remember that all information provided is strictly confidential.

In the past 5 years, has your current spouse/partner threatened to hit you with his/her fist or anything else that could have hurt you?

During the past 5 years, has he/she thrown anything at you that could have hurt you?

During the past 5 years, has he/she pushed, grabbed or shoved you in a way that could have hurt you?

During the past 5 years, has he/she slapped you?

During the past 5 years, has he/she kicked you, bit you, or hit you with his/her fist?

During the past 5 years, has he/she hit you with something that could have hurt you?

During the past 5 years, has he/she beaten you?

During the past 5 years, has he/she choked you?

During the past 5 years, has he/she used or threatened to use a gun or knife on you?

During the past 5 years, has he/she forced you into any unwanted sexual activity, by threatening you, holding you down, or hurting you in some way?

Source: General Social Survey, *Cycle 18—Victimization, Main Survey—Questionnaire Package* (Ottawa: Statistics Canada, Housing, Family and Social Statistics Division, 2004).

agencies, reasons that they did or did not report their victimization, and the extent of use of a range of social services. Researchers are often also interested in victims' attitudes toward various components of the criminal justice system, including police and courts, as well as their fear of crime.

Nevertheless, victimization surveys, as all research tools, have limitations that must be borne in mind when assessing their use and the data that emerge from them. Some of the more salient ones are outlined below.

Competing Definitions of Crime: One of the main challenges of victimization surveys is to use language and terminology that are both meaningful to victims and comparable to official definitions of crime. Anyone who has flipped through the *Criminal Code* will see that it would be ill advised to rely on legal terminology when interviewing people in the community. Indeed, we may not always want to limit ourselves to official definitions of crime as they fail to capture many experiences (e.g., emotional abuse) that are not criminal in law. Nevertheless, one of the main purposes of carrying out victimization surveys is to compare official rates with unofficial rates. Without points of comparison, this task becomes impossible.

Inaccurate Reporting by the Victim/Respondent: There are a number of ways in which the respondents' answers may be inaccurate. For example, there is a tendency to report events that occurred more recently (e.g., last week) than ones that occurred some time ago (e.g., last year). In addition, "telescoping — the tendency of respondents to move forward and report as having occurred events that actually took place before the reference period" (Hagan, 2000, p. 196), may also occur. For example, if the survey question refers to events that occurred within the last six months, respondents may inadvertently report on events that occurred four months previous to that, inadvertently distorting the findings to some degree. Finally, victims may, as with police-reported data, underreport more minor offences and offences in which the assailant was a friend, relative, or family member (Hagan, 2000).

Limited Scope of Victimization Surveys: An important criticism of victimization surveys is that they tend to focus only on certain types of victimization and are not well suited for others. For example, "sensitive" crimes, such as offences against children (Macmillan et al., 1996) are rarely included. Indeed, there are legal and ethical dilemmas in using victimization surveys to measure violence against children. More specifically, the integrity of the surveys depends on assurances of confidentiality and anonymity to respondents. However, researchers who come into possession of knowledge about abuse of children may be under a legal duty to report the abuse to the authorities. Fitzgerald (1999) suggests there may be similar complications in measuring abuse against dependent adults in some provinces.

In addition, however, there are whole categories of offences, many involving violence, which victimization surveys do not and perhaps cannot measure. Homicides, crimes against businesses, and a full range of "victimless" offences (e.g., drug use or prostitution) cannot be assessed with this tool (Ogrodnik and Trainor, 1997). In addition, "how the state (including the law) actively contributes to the victims we see or do not see" (Walklate, 2000, p. 186) is masked through traditional definitions and methods of measurement. For example, "[a]s with the UCR, victim surveys do not concern themselves particularly with corporate, occupational, organized, professional, political and public order crimes" (Hagan, 2000, p. 196). State violence, such as police brutality, and violence against those in state institutions are rarely included.

Walklate (2000) notes that victimization surveys cannot capture "the deeply embedded nature of social relationships which feed into anyone's experience of personal safety, but women's in particular" (p. 88). While the Violence Against Women Survey conducted by Statistics Canada (1993) was designed to overcome the limitations of traditional survey techniques in uncovering the nature and complexity of violence against women in intimate partner relationships, "[t]he arbitrary assignment of 'victim' status to women who have been sexually or physically assaulted in the previous year and 'nonvictim' status to those not victimized very recently mis-classifies many women" (Johnson, 1998, p. 26). The early criticisms that relate to the relationship between victimization and race, class, and gender remain (DeKeseredy and MacLean, 1991).

The methodological limitations associated with victimization surveys are not insurmountable. As with all research tools, they must be assessed in the context of the particular research agenda and the costs and benefits associated with the various methods available. They have emerged as a critical tool to victimologists, but one that should not escape scrutiny. A central question must be whether the benefits outweigh the limitations, and whether they result in useful, meaningful, and valuable data that would otherwise be lost, particularly in light of the traditional and entrenched reliance on police-reported data.

ALTERNATIVE METHODS OF MEASURING VICTIMIZATION

SELF-REPORT SURVEYS

There are alternative, indirect ways in which we may be able to measure victimization. One approach, again more commonly employed to measure criminality, is the self-report survey in which individuals are asked about their own criminal behaviour. These studies are generally designed to uncover a broader range of information about crime than is available through police-reported data. Indeed, they are designed to include those crimes and other behaviours that may not be reported. Studies of this type were originally carried out on juveniles and consistently reported a high level of involvement of young people in a wide range of activities from very minor to quite serious criminal behaviours (Gabor, 1994). Most of these never came to the attention of the police. Examples of self-report studies include the ongoing research by the Canadian Association of Mental Health on drug, tobacco, and alcohol use by high-school students and adults in Ontario (Adlaf and Paglia, 2003). (See Box 3.3)

Self-report studies share some characteristics with victimization surveys: They are typically anonymous and confidential, and they may be administered in a number of ways, such as over the phone or through the mail. They may ask respondents whether they have committed particular acts within a specified time frame, and whether they were caught. For example, a survey of dating behaviour on Canadian university campuses found significant numbers of men who admitted abusing their girlfriends either emotionally, physically, or sexually (DeKeseredy and Schwartz, 1998). In reporting on data collected for the National Longitudinal Survey on Children and Youth, Sprott et al. (2001) report on aggressive behaviour by 10- and 11-year-olds, which included acts of "physically attacking someone." While these types of data are clearly more limited in what they reveal about victimization, particularly from the perspective of the victim, they may serve as yet one more piece of the puzzle.

Some may question whether respondents will answer honestly when being asked about their own criminal or delinquent behaviour. As Sprott et al. (2001) report, there is generally a strong relationship between self-reports of delinquency and official police records. Perhaps a greater problem with this type of instrument is that they generally focus on more minor types of crime and, like victimization surveys, underestimate more serious crimes, including those involving violence.

INSTITUTIONAL DATA

The victimization of certain populations creates significant challenges for measuring victimization. Due to their dependent and vulnerable situation, children, the elderly, and those in living in institutions are perhaps the best examples. Victimization at the hands of the parents or primary caretakers, either in the home or in institutional settings, generally takes place in private, out of the scrutiny of those who might report it.

Box 3.3: Student Questionnaire

These questions are to find out what students, like yourself, know about alcohol and other drugs (for example, tobacco, cannabis, hallucinogens, cocaine, heroin, and medical drugs); how you feel about alcohol and other drugs; and what you do about using alcohol and other drugs. There is no assumption that students who answer the questionnaire have ever used alcohol or other drugs. Do NOT put your name on the questionnaire. The information you give is to be kept completely secret and confidential. We ask you, therefore, to be completely honest and accurate when you answer the questions. If you do not wish to answer a question, leave it blank. Also, you may withdraw from the survey at any time. THANK YOU FOR YOUR HELP.

THE NEXT FEW QUESTIONS ARE ABOUT CANNABIS. PLEASE ANSWER ALL QUESTIONS, EVEN IF YOU HAVE NEVER USED CANNABIS.

When (if ever) did you first try CANNABIS (also known as marijuana, "weed," "grass," "pot," hashish, "hash," hash oil)?

During the LAST 4 WEEKS how often (if ever) did you use cannabis (also known as marijuana, "weed," "grass," "pot," hashish, "hash," hash oil)?

During the LAST 4 WEEKS, on occasions when you have used marijuana, how many joints did you typically smoke? (If you shared joints with others, count only the amount that YOU smoked.)

In the LAST 12 MONTHS, have you tried to stop using marijuana or hashish but found that you couldn't stop?

In the LAST 12 MONTHS, has there been a period when you used marijuana or hashish every day or almost every day for at least a month?

In the LAST 12 MONTHS, have you tried to cut down your use of marijuana or hashish?

How many of your CLOSEST friends use marijuana or hashish?

How often (if ever) in the last 12 months have you done each of the following?

Taken a car for a ride without the owner's permission?

Banged up or damaged something (on purpose) that did not belong to you?

Sold marijuana or hashish?

Taken things worth $50 or less that did not belong to you?

Taken things worth more than $50 that did not belong to you?

Beat up or hurt anyone (on purpose), not counting fights with a brother or sister?

Broken into a locked building other than your own home?

Carried a weapon, such as a gun or knife?

Sold drugs other than marijuana or hashish?

Taken part in gang fights?

Were thrown out of your home (that is, you were told to leave your home when you did not want to leave)?

Run away from home (that is, left home without the permission of one or both of your parents)?

Carried a handgun?

Source: Centre for Addiction and Mental Health, *2005 Student Drug Questionnaire* (Toronto: Centre for Addition and Mental Health, 2005).

In the case of children, there are additional complicating factors that prevent their victimization from becoming known. The home is seen as the impenetrable realm of the parents, and the state and its agencies (including the police and child welfare agencies) have limited jurisdiction to intervene. Indeed, Macmillan et al. (1996) estimate that roughly 90 percent of cases of child abuse go unreported to child welfare agencies. In addition, however, children are treated as less credible witnesses than adults due to their limited verbal and cognitive abilities. This leads to difficulties in substantiating and prosecuting allegations.

Depending on the specifics of the situation, the elderly may share some of the same challenges and barriers to having their victimizations responded to in a meaningful way. They are often vulnerable to their caretakers (be they family or paid workers), their memory may be problematic, they may injure more easily, and they often have limited access to the outside world and agencies who may intervene.

It is in this context that institutional data become valuable. That is, the various social, health, and community institutions that provide direct services to people who may be victims of crime are important sources of otherwise unavailable data. For example, Trocmé et al. (2003) report on the nature and extent of child maltreatment as revealed through the Canadian Incident Study of Reported Child Abuse and Neglect, which relied on data from child welfare investigators about cases of reported child abuse or neglect. From this, the authors could assess the nature and extent of suspected and substantiated cases of child "maltreatment." However, this, too, relied on reporting to child welfare authorities. Like victimization reported to the police, it results in a highly filtered subset of cases.

Emergency departments in hospitals may also provide valuable data on victimization from injured individuals who go to hospital emergency rooms for treatment (Rand, 1997). While the possible causes of those injuries are vast and most will not relate to criminal activity, they likely include a certain number of people whose injuries are a direct result of family violence, gang violence, or drinking and driving, as examples. Hospital staff may obtain relevant information from the patient or individuals accompanying the patient. Clearly, some of these incidents will make their way into official police statistics, but a great many will not. Indeed, the Ontario government has introduced legislation to make it mandatory for doctors to report to police any patients with gunshot wounds who attend emergency rooms in Ontario (Ministry of Community Safety and Correctional Services, 2003). Additionally, in some cases, such as suspected child abuse, hospital medical personnel are required by law to report such cases to child welfare authorities.

A perhaps different source of institutional data comes not from service agencies but from the very institutions in which victims or potential victims may reside. These populations are generally structurally excluded from most surveys regardless of the particular reason for their living situation. So, for example, the experiences of elderly residents of nursing or retirement homes, individuals of any age in hospitals or other care facilities, and adults and youth in correctional centres are absent despite their higher risk for victimization from both their caretakers and other residents. Researchers may be denied access to either the whole population or important data, or residents may be fearful of participating. Those who do participate may constitute a highly skewed, non-representative sample.

However, it is possible to design methodologies and instruments specifically for institutionalized populations. For example, *Voices From Within: Youth Speak Out* (Snow and Finlay, 1998) provides data on the views and experiences of youth in custodial settings, such as foster care, Children's Aid Society group homes, children's mental health centres, or shelters. While the themes of the research are broad, there are considerable data on staff's use of physical restraint and force against youth in custody.

CHALLENGING MEASUREMENTS: SYSTEMIC FORMS OF VICTIMIZATION

Perhaps one of the most intractable challenges of measuring victimization rests with systemic forms of victimization. Such incidents are not isolated, with a single perpetrator and a single victim. Indeed, many argue that racism, violence against women and children, and hate crimes are forms of victimization that are entrenched in social systems and often supported by the state explicitly or in more subtle ways. However, they are less commonly measured as official forms of victimization as, say, robbery or assault, which occur on the street.

There are mechanisms that are often used to go beyond individual incidents to examine patterns of behaviour and their causal roots. For example, coroner's inquests are often called into "suspicious" or high-profile deaths to find out the "who, what, where, when, and how." While inquests cannot make findings of criminality, they have the advantage of hearing testimony under oath about the broader systemic roots of an incident in a forum where many of the legal barriers to admitting evidence and giving testimony are relaxed.

For example, in the murder–suicide of Arlene May and Randy Iles in March 1996, in which Randy Iles murdered his ex-common-law wife and then killed himself, criminal charges were clearly irrelevant. However, in spite of his history of domestic violence and a bail condition requiring him to surrender any firearms, Randy Iles was able to purchase a gun. He held Arlene May and her three children hostage in their own home. While the children were allowed to leave, neither Arlene May nor Randy Iles survived. The coroner's inquest, which was held into this tragedy, heard testimony from 76 witnesses over 51 days. The jury made over 100 recommendations (Coroner's Office, 1998), covering everything from the police risk assessment of domestic violence incidents to tighter controls on the issuance of Firearms Acquisitions Certificates by individuals convicted of domestic violence. While the recommendations are not binding on any of the parties, they can often lead to significant policy and legal reform.

What, then, is the best way to measure victimization? This question must be approached the same way we might approach the study of other social phenomena. Researchers often rely on "triangulation" or a variety of methodologies, each of which approaches the topic from a different vantage point, but will come together to paint a picture that is fuller than the one achieved when relying on only one approach. This is "a position which recognizes that different research techniques can uncover different layers of social reality and that the role of the researcher is to look for confirmations and contradictions between those different layers of information" (Walklate, 2000, p. 191). In the chapters that follow, we will present victimization data from a variety of sources that reflect the most current available Canadian data, and that rely primarily on a combination of victimization and police-reported data. It will be followed by a more focused discussion of the limitations of applying these methods to systemic forms of victimization, particularly with respect to Aboriginal peoples and the situation of hate crimes in Canada.

QUESTIONS FOR FURTHER CONSIDERATION

1. Discuss the strengths and weaknesses of each method to measure the following, and suggest which one you think is best in each situation:
   (a) gang violence
   (b) sexual assaults
   (c) victimization among the homeless

General Patterns of Victimization in Canada

THIS CHAPTER WILL present findings on patterns of victimization in Canada. Deciding precisely which data to present and from which source is always difficult. This is particularly true when there is no single focus on particular forms of victimization, such as family or sexual violence, which might define the parameters more clearly. The goal here is not to provide a comprehensive and detailed presentation of all forms of victimization; that would be a mundane task for the reader and be of little analytic value. In keeping with the broader themes of the text, instead we present in this chapter a general overview of the nature of violent victimization in Canada. In the chapter which follows, we present the most recent data on patterns of family violence, including spousal violence, and family violence against children and older adults.

An additional challenge in any such exercise is identifying the most reliable data available. Due to their relative strengths, victimization data from the most recent General Social Survey (Au Coin, 2005b; Gannon and Mihorean, 2005) will provide the primary source of information. (See Box 4.1)

While the limitations of police-reported data are perhaps significant (see Chapter 3), the breadth, currency, and availability of such data make it difficult to exclude them, particularly in the absence of victimization data. The specific source of the data presented here will be clearly identified. The reader is reminded to interpret the data with the appropriate methodological limitations in mind.

Box 4.1: Methodology

In 2004, Statistics Canada conducted the victimization cycle of the General Social Survey for the fourth time. Previous cycles were conducted in 1988, 1993, and 1999. The objectives of the survey are to provide estimates of the extent to which people experience incidences of eight offence types, examine risk factors associated with victimization, examine reporting rates to police, and measure fear of crime and public perceptions of crime and the criminal justice system.

Sampling
Households in the 10 provinces were selected using Random Digit Dialing (RDD). Once a household was chosen, an individual 15 years or older was selected randomly to respond to the survey. Households without telephones, households with only cellular phone service, and individuals living in institutions were excluded. These groups combined represented 4 percent of the target population. This figure is not large enough to significantly change the estimates.

The sample size in 2004 was about 24,000 households, similar to the sample size in 1999 (26,000) and considerably higher than the sample in 1993 and 1988 (10,000 each).

Data Collection
Data collection took place from January to December 2004 inclusively. The sample was evenly distributed over the 12 months to represent seasonal variation in the information. A standard questionnaire was conducted by phone using computer-assisted telephone interviewing (CATI). A typical interview lasted 30 minutes.

Response Rates
Of the 31,895 households that were selected for the GSS Cycle 18 sample, 23,766 usable responses were obtained. This represents a response rate of 75 percent. Types of non-responses included respondents who refused to participate, could not be reached, or could not speak English or French.

Respondents in the sample were weighted so that their responses represent the non-institutionalized Canadian population aged 15 years or over. Each person who responded to the 2004 GSS represented roughly 1,000 people in the Canadian population aged 15 years and over.

Data Limitations
As with any household survey, there are some data limitations. The results are based on a sample and are therefore subject to sampling error. Somewhat different results might have been obtained if the entire population had been surveyed. The difference between the estimate obtained from the sample and the one resulting

CHAPTER 4

from a complete count is called the sampling error of the estimate. This Juristat uses the coefficient of variation (CV) as a measure of the sampling error. Any estimate that has a high CV (over 33.3 percent) has not been published because the estimate is too unreliable. In these cases, the symbol F is used in the figures and data tables. An estimate that has a CV between 16.6 and 33.3 should be used with caution and the symbol E is used.

Source: Maire Gannon and Karen Mihorean, "Criminal Victimization in Canada, 2005," *Juristat* 25(7) (2005). Statistics Canada.

GENERAL PATTERNS OF VICTIMIZATION

The 2004 General Social Survey (Gannon and Mihorean, 2005) measured victimization with respect to three categories of crime: violent victimizations (i.e., sexual assault, robbery, physical assault), theft of personal property (not including robbery, which includes violence or the threat of violence), and household victimizations (i.e., break and enter, motor vehicle/parts theft, theft of household property, and vandalism). In cases of multiple offences during the same incident, victimizations were classified according to the most serious offence.

Twenty-eight percent of Canadians aged 15 or older living in the 10 provinces reported that they were victimized one or more times in the 12 months preceding the survey; most of these involved household crimes. (See Figure 4.1)

There was no statistically significant change in the rate of violent incidents from the 1999 General Social Survey (at 111 per 1,000 population) to the 2004 General Social Survey (at 106 per 1,000 population; see Besserer and Trainor, 2000, for more detailed findings from the 1999 General Social Survey). However, the rate of household victimizations increased from 218 per 1,000 households in Canada in 1999 to 248 victimizations per 1,000 households in 2004. The rate of personal property theft increased from 75 per 1,000 population in 1999 to 93 per 1,000 population in 2004.

Differences in rates of victimization were reported that relate to gender, sexuality, and age. For example, women and men were at similar risk of victimization, at 102 per 1,000 women and 111 per 1,000 men.

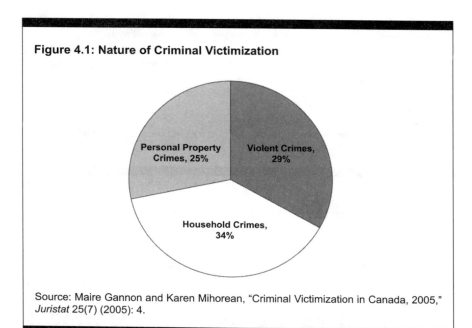

Figure 4.1: Nature of Criminal Victimization

Personal Property Crimes, 25%

Violent Crimes, 29%

Household Crimes, 34%

Source: Maire Gannon and Karen Mihorean, "Criminal Victimization in Canada, 2005," *Juristat* 25(7) (2005): 4.

There were, however, significant differences in the types of victimizations experienced by women and men: sexual assaults were five times higher for women, while men were more likely to report physical assaults and robbery. (See Figure 4.2)

Respondents who identified themselves as either gay or lesbian reported violent victimizations at a rate of 242 per 1,000 population compared to 99 per 1,000 population for respondents who identified themselves as heterosexual, a rate that is 2.5 times higher (Gannon and Mihorean, 2005). At the same time, younger people were at a generally higher risk of victimization.

The greatest risk of personal victimization was for people between the ages of 15–24, a rate 1.5 times higher than those in other age groups. Indeed, people over 65 had the lowest rate of personal victimization, at 12 incidents per 1,000 population. (See Table 4.1)

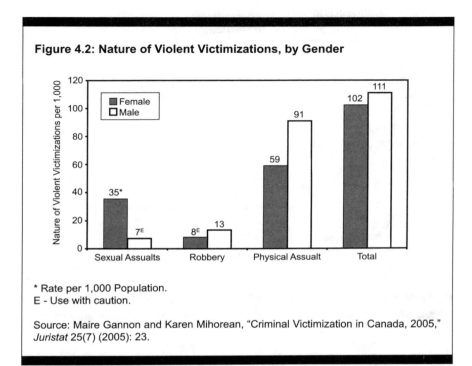

Figure 4.2: Nature of Violent Victimizations, by Gender

* Rate per 1,000 Population.
E - Use with caution.

Source: Maire Gannon and Karen Mihorean, "Criminal Victimization in Canada, 2005," *Juristat* 25(7) (2005): 23.

The General Social Survey, as with other victimization surveys, also looks at victimization as a function of a variety of social characteristics. Those who are single were at elevated risk of violent victimizations compared to those in common-law relationships and those who are married.[1] (See Figure 4.3)

The data also indicated that those looking for work and students had the highest rates of violent victimization, while the lowest rates were among those who were retired. (See Figure 4.4) Those from households with incomes less than $15,000 were most likely to be victims. (See Figure 4.5)

Table 4.1: Nature of Violent Victimizations, by Age*

Age	Sexual Assault	Robbery	Physical Assault	Total
15–24 years	57	33	136	226
25–34 years	30	10ᴱ	116	157
35–44 years	20	8ᴱ	87	115
45–54 years	8ᴱ	6ᴱ	48	62
55–64 years	7ᴱ	F	36ᴱ	45
65+ years	7ᴱ	F	10ᴱ	12ᴱ

* Rate per 1,000.
E - Use with caution.
F - Too unreliable to be published.

Source: Maire Gannon and Karen Mihorean, "Criminal Victimization in Canada, 2005," *Juristat* 25(7) (2005): 23.

Figure 4.3: Rate of Violent Victimizations, by Marital Status*

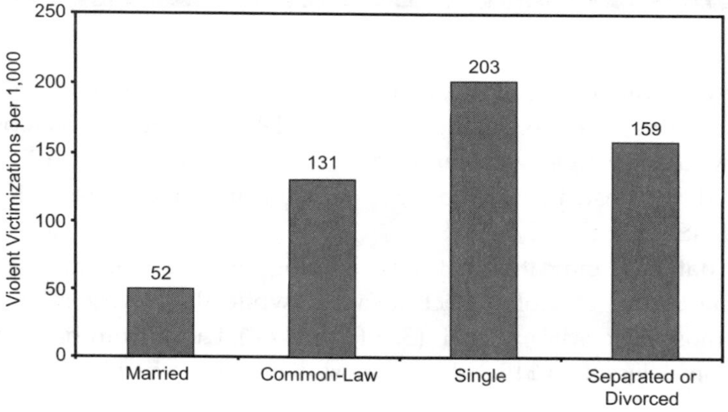

* Data for those who are widowed are too unreliable to report

Source: Maire Gannon and Karen Mihorean, "Criminal Victimization in Canada, 2005," *Juristat* 25(7) (2005): 230.

Figure 4.4: Rate of Violent Victimizations, by Main Activity*

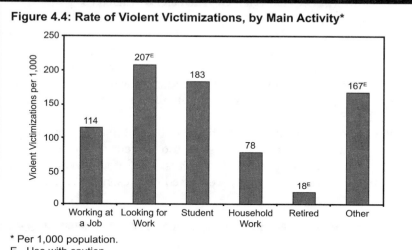

* Per 1,000 population.
E - Use with caution.

Source: Maire Gannon and Karen Mihorean, "Criminal Victimization in Canada, 2005," *Juristat* 25(7) (2005): 23.

Figure 4.5: Rate of Violent Victimizations, by Income*

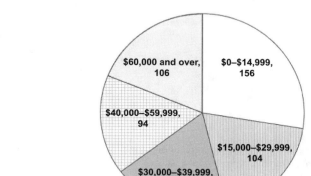

* Per 1,000 population

Source: Maire Gannon and Karen Mihorean, "Criminal Victimization in Canada, 2005," *Juristat* 25(7) (2005): 23.

CHARACTERISTICS OF VIOLENT INCIDENTS

The General Social Survey provides limited information on the context of violent incidents (Gannon and Mihorean, 2005), including characteristics of perpetrators of these acts. For example, 38 percent of violent incidents (excluding spousal assaults) occurred in a commercial or public institution, such as an office, factory, store, shopping mall, bar or restaurant, school, or a hospital. (See Figure 4.6)

One-quarter of violent victimizations involved the use or presence of a weapon: knives were used or present in 6 percent of incidents; guns were used or present in 3 percent of incidents; and "other" weapons, such as bottles, bats, sticks, and rocks, were used or present in 17 percent of incidents.

Figure 4.6: Location of Violent Victimizations*

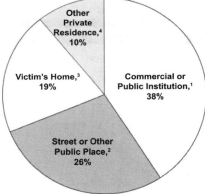

* Excludes incidents of spousal sexual and physical assault.
1 - Includes restaurant/bar, factory, shopping mall, school.
2 - Includes public transportation, parking lots, streets.
3 - Includes inside home or apartment, vacation property, yard, farm.
4 - Includes in or around offender's home or other private residence.

Source: Maire Gannon and Karen Mihorean, "Criminal Victimization in Canada, 2005," *Juristat* 25(7) (2005): 9.

Over three-quarters of violent incidents involved one accused, 87 percent of whom were male. The majority were young, that is, between the ages of 12–17 years old. While older males were less frequently involved as accused, 40 percent of individuals accused of sexual assaults were 35 years of age or older compared to 31 percent of those accused of physical assaults and 26 percent of those accused of robberies.

Overall, for those incidents involving a lone accused, the accused was known to the victim in 51 percent of incidents, while the accused was a stranger in 44 percent of incidents and a family member in 5 percent of incidents. The accused was a friend or acquaintance in 64 percent of sexual assaults and 49 percent of physical assaults. In contrast, the accused in incidents of robbery was a stranger in 60 percent of incidents.

Responding to Victimization

One of the main ways we rely on to understand criminal victimization is through victims' disclosure about the incident. There is a wide range of individuals, services, or institutions in the community that might offer support after a victimization. Indeed, according to the 2004 General Social Survey, victims of violent incidents discussed the incident with friends or neighbours in 75 percent of these incidents, and with family members in 60 percent of these incidents. Overall, victims turned to professional or community resources in 9 percent of victimizations: this was the case for 13 percent of sexual assault victims compared to 7 percent of victims of physical assault. At the same time, 7 percent of victims of violent incidents told no one about their experience before disclosing to the interviewer during the administration of the survey.

The option of reporting their victimization to police is an important alternative for victims. In addition, the significant role of police-reported crime statistics in shaping our response to crime and victimization makes understanding the non-reporting of such incidents particularly valuable. According to the 2004 General Social Survey, 33 percent of violent victimizations were reported to the police. Robberies (at 46 percent) and physical assaults (at 39 percent) were the most likely to be reported, while sexual assaults were the least likely to be reported, at 8 percent. (See Figure 4.7)

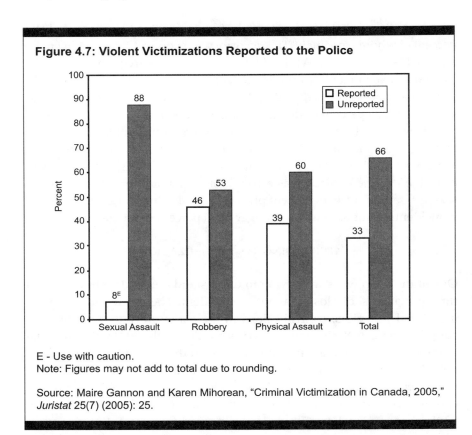

Figure 4.7: Violent Victimizations Reported to the Police

E - Use with caution.
Note: Figures may not add to total due to rounding.

Source: Maire Gannon and Karen Mihorean, "Criminal Victimization in Canada, 2005," *Juristat* 25(7) (2005): 25.

Victims gave a wide range of reasons for reporting their experience to the police: 83 percent stated it was their duty to report the incident to the police, 74 percent stated that they wanted the offender arrested or punished, and 70 percent stated that they wanted to stop the violence or wanted protection from the offender. Twenty percent stated that they reported their victimization to the police to make an insurance claim or receive compensation, and 19 percent stated they did so on someone else's recommendation.

There are certain characteristics of the incident that influence a victim's decision to report the incident to the police. For example, victimizations that resulted in injury to the victims were reported 47 percent of the time (compared to 28 percent of incidents in which there was no injury to the victims); victimizations involving a weapon were reported 53 percent of the time (compared to 25 percent of incidents in which no weapon was used); and victimizations in which the victims had to take time off work were reported to the police 51 percent of the time (compared to 27 percent of incidents in which the victims did not take time off work).

At the same time, 60 percent of incidents were not reported to the police because the victims dealt with it another way; 53 percent of incidents were not reported to the police because, according to the victims, it was not important enough; and 42 percent were not reported to the police because the victims did not want the police involved. Thirty-nine percent stated they felt it was a personal matter, and 29 percent stated that they didn't think the police could do anything about it. In 11 percent of cases the victim stated that the victimization was not reported to the police because they feared the offender would retaliate.

THINKING ABOUT VIOLENT VICTIMIZATION

Given the range and complexity of the victimizations presented above, a detailed analysis of the findings would not be feasible. However, the data do beg certain questions, which are hinted at through the emergence of "patterned" victimizations. For example, when collapsed over categories, we see that violent crimes (excluding forms of spousal and family violence) are not the most prevalent of the categories included in the survey, despite popular and politicized messages about the threats to personal safety in the community. At the same time, alarming patterns emerge when we tease out gender, sexuality, and age. We also have strong hints about the depth of the relationship between victims and perpetrators, and the prevalence of men throughout the victimization experience. No doubt had the survey included measures of race and ethnicity, for example, we might have evidence of additional "risk" factors. This highlights both the value of existing measures (we have indeed learned a lot), as well as the limitations of current tools, since there is more to be uncovered as they evolve.

NOTE

1.   Excludes spousal assault. See Gannon and Mihorean (2005) for a discussion of the rationale for this analysis.

QUESTIONS FOR FURTHER CONSIDERATION

1. Are there some findings about the nature and patterns of criminal victimization that surprise you? Which ones? Discuss why.
2. What factors might explain the "risk" associated with the higher rates of victimization linked to some activities?

CHAPTER 5

Patterns of Violence within the Family in Canada

AS REINFORCED throughout this text, it is important to pay attention to the specific research instruments when collecting or analyzing data. As Fitzgerald (1999) points out, victimization surveys designed specifically to measure family violence may result in higher estimates of its occurrence in the community since they are designed to focus more directly on that experience. In addition, the breadth of the definitions used in the survey may also influence the findings. For example, broad definitions of "family," which include marriage, adoption, foster care, and "step and blended family arrangements" (p. 9), will result in higher reporting. Similarly, broad definitions of "violence," which go beyond physical attacks to include threats of violence and physical and emotional abuse, will also increase estimates. This is not, in and of itself, problematic as the results are likely more reflective of the range of violent experiences in victims' lives. However, it may make comparison with other sources of data problematic.

Through a variety of tools over the past few decades, Statistics Canada has been tracking the nature and extent of violence between couples in intimate, spousal relationships (e.g., Au Coin 2005b; Pottie Bunge and Locke, 2000; Statistics Canada, 1993). The most recent General Social Survey, conducted in 2004, continued with this as one theme. In this chapter, we present the most recent Canadian victimization data on violence in family relationships, including between spouses, and involving both children and older adults.

SPOUSAL VIOLENCE

For the 2004 General Social Survey (Mihorean, 2005b), respondents who were married or living common-law at the time of the survey were deemed to be in a "spousal relationship" and were questioned about both physical and sexual violence. Responses indicate that, while both women and men report similar rates of violence in their current relationships, "women continue to suffer more serious and repeated spousal violence than do men and incur more serious consequences as a result of this violence" (Mihorean, 2005b, p. 13).

For example, 3 percent of women and 4 percent of men in current marital or common-law relationships reported either physical or sexual violence from their partners. While both women and men were most likely to report being shoved, grabbed, or slapped, women were more likely to report being beaten, choked, threatened with a gun or knife, or had a gun or knife used against them than were men. (See Figure 5.1)

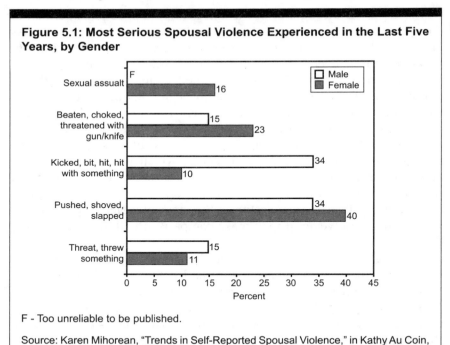

Figure 5.1: Most Serious Spousal Violence Experienced in the Last Five Years, by Gender

F - Too unreliable to be published.

Source: Karen Mihorean, "Trends in Self-Reported Spousal Violence," in Kathy Au Coin, ed., *Family Violence in Canada: A Statistical Profile 2005* (Ottawa: Minister of Industry, Statistics Canada, Canadian Centre for Justice Statistics, 2005), 15.

Sixteen percent of women reported that sexual assault was the most serious violence they experienced at the hands of their partners; the number of men who fall into this category is too small to provide a reliable estimate.

Gender-specific patterns of spousal violence are also found in the number of violent incidents experienced by women versus men, as well as the consequences of the violence. Fifty-four percent of those who experienced spousal violence responded that it occurred on more than one occasion. (See Figure 5.2) Forty percent of women and 48 percent of men stated that it occurred once, while 21 percent of women and 11 percent of men reported that it had occurred more than 10 times. Not surprisingly, then, women are more likely to report injury as a result of the violence.

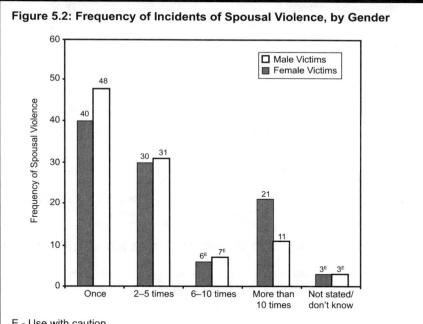

Figure 5.2: Frequency of Incidents of Spousal Violence, by Gender

E - Use with caution.

Source: Karen Mihorean, "Trends in Self-Reported Spousal Violence," in Kathy Au Coin, ed., *Family Violence in Canada: A Statistical Profile 2005* (Ottawa: Minister of Industry, Statistics Canada, Canadian Centre for Justice Statistics, 2005), 29.

One-quarter of all respondents who had experienced violence in their intimate relationship reported fearing for their lives. However, women were afraid for their lives in 34 percent of the cases, and men feared for their lives in 10 percent of the cases. (See Table 5.1)

Table 5.1: Severity of Spousal Violence, by Gender

Severity of Violence	Female (%)	Male (%)
Physical injury	44	19
No physical injury	56	81
Not stated/don't know	F	F
Received medical attention	13	2[E]
Did not receive medical attention	30	16
No physical injury	56	81
Not stated/don't know	F	F
Feared for their life	34	10
Did not fear for their life	65	90
Not stated/don't know	F	F

Percentages may not total 100 percent due to rounding.
E—Use with caution.
F—Too unreliable to publish.

Source: Karen Mihorean, "Trends in Self-Reported Spousal Violence," in Kathy Au Coin, ed., *Family Violence in Canada: A Statistical Profile 2005* (Ottawa: Minister of Industry, Statistics Canada, Canadian Centre for Justice Statistics, 2005), 30.

The General Social Survey provides strong data on the risk factors that are related to spousal violence. (See Figure 5.2) The most recent data support findings from earlier surveys:

> ... spousal violence affects all socio-demographic groups. However, there are certain segments of the population that are more vulnerable to spousal violence than others. As indicated below, those who are young, who live in a common-law relationship, who have been in the relationship for

Table 5.2: Spousal Violence by Personal Characteristics of Victims, by Gender

| | Sex of Victim | |
	Female % of Population	Male % of Population
Total violence by a current partner	1	2
Age group of victim		
Under 25	F	F
25–34	2E	4
35–44	2E	1E
45–54	1E	F
55 and over	1E	1E
Type of union		
Married	1	1
Common-law	3E	4
Household income		
Less than $30,000	2E	F
$30,000–$59,999	2E	2E
$60,000 or more	1E	2E
Not stated/don't know	F	F
Education of victim		
Less than high school	F	F
High-school diploma	1E	F
Some post secondary[1]	1E	2
University degree	1E	2E
Not stated/don't know	F	F
Education of spouse/partner		
Less than high school	2E	F
High-school diploma	F	2E
Some post-secondary[1]	2E	2E
University degree	1E	2E
Not stated/don't know	F	F

E – Use with caution.
F – Too unreliable to be published.
1 – Some post-secondary includes diploma, a certification from a community college, or a trade/technical college.

Source: Karen Mihorean, "Trends in Self-Reported Spousal Violence," in Kathy Au Coin, ed., *Family Violence in Canada: A Statistical Profile 2005* (Ottawa: Minister of Industry, Statistics Canada, Canadian Centre for Justice Statistics, 2005), 31.

three years or less, who are Aboriginal, and whose partner is a frequent heavy drinker are at increased risk of experiencing violence at the hands of their intimate partner. (Mihorean, 2005b, p. 17)

One persistent finding in the spousal violence literature is that emotional abuse often precedes or co-occurs with violence in intimate relationships (Pottie Bunge, 2000). These data provide additional support for this. Eighteen percent of women and 17 percent of men reported emotional abuse in a current or previous spousal relationship (either marriage or common-law). However, 13 percent of women versus 7 percent of men reported that their partners put them down or called them names to make them feel bad, 3 percent of women and 1 percent of men reported that their partners threatened to harm someone close to them, and 4 percent of women and 2 percent of men reported that their partners prevented them from having access to the family income even when they asked for it.

RESPONDING TO SPOUSAL VIOLENCE

As with the general data on violent victimization presented in Chapter 4, we find that both female and male victims of spousal violence respond in a variety of ways, many of which do not involve the criminal justice system, including police. Seventy-three percent of all victims of spousal violence confided in someone close to them about their victimization. Women turned to informal sources of help (such as a doctor or nurse) 83 percent of the time, while men turned to informal sources of help 60 percent of the time. Both women (at 67 percent) and men (at 44 percent) frequently turned to family members, followed by friends and neighbours (for 63 percent of females and 41 percent of males).

Professional services also play a role here. Thirty-four percent of both women and men turned to a formal agency for help; 28 percent turned to a counsellor or psychologist; 10 percent turned to a crisis centre or crisis line; 9 percent turned to a community or family centre; and 5 percent turned to victim-based services. Those who did not turn to a formal social service agency most frequently stated that they didn't do so because they did not want or need help from such an agency (48 percent of females and 55 percent of males), the incident was too minor (21 percent of females and 29 percent of males), and because they didn't know of such services or such services weren't available (5 percent of females and 7 percent of males).

Twenty-eight percent of respondents who reported at least one act of spousal violence in the previous five years stated that the incident had come to the attention of the police. This was true for 36 percent of the women, but only 17 percent of men. Indeed, men reported the violence against them to the police in 51 percent of the cases, while this was true for women in 75 percent of the cases. At the same time, over 60 percent of victims experienced more than one violent incident before contact with the police, and just under half experienced more than 10 incidents before contact with the police.

Over half of both women and men stated that they contacted the police because it was their duty to do so. (See Figure 5.3) Eighty-eight percent of

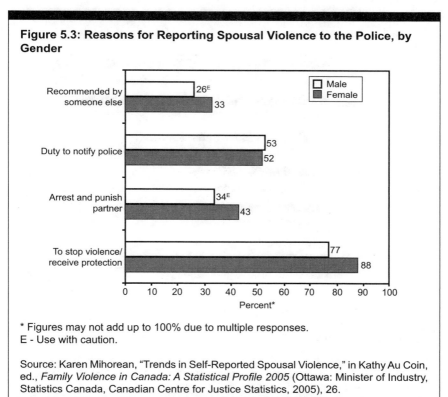

Figure 5.3: Reasons for Reporting Spousal Violence to the Police, by Gender

* Figures may not add up to 100% due to multiple responses.
E - Use with caution.

Source: Karen Mihorean, "Trends in Self-Reported Spousal Violence," in Kathy Au Coin, ed., *Family Violence in Canada: A Statistical Profile 2005* (Ottawa: Minister of Industry, Statistics Canada, Canadian Centre for Justice Statistics, 2005), 26.

women and 77 percent of men stated that they contacted the police to stop the violence and to receive protection, and 43 percent of women and 34 percent of men stated that they contacted the police to have their abusive partner arrested and punished.

On the other hand, victims gave a range of reasons for *not* contacting the police: they didn't want anyone to find out about the abuse (at 35 percent); it was dealt with another way (at 21 percent); or the victim felt it was a personal matter that did not concern the police (at 14 percent). Of interest to note is that 22 percent of victims overall had not told anyone of their abuse before participating in the survey, which included 12 percent of female victims and 35 percent of male victims.

Victims were also asked about the action taken by the police when they were called as a result of their spousal abuse. (See Figure 5.4) In 82

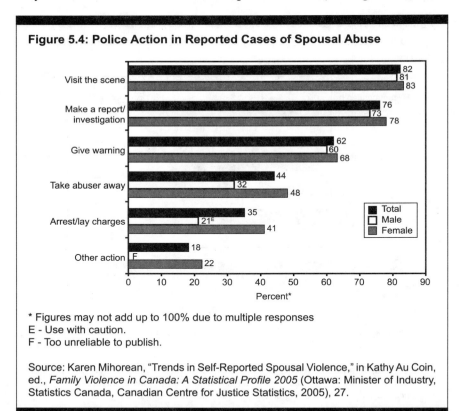

Figure 5.4: Police Action in Reported Cases of Spousal Abuse

* Figures may not add up to 100% due to multiple responses
E - Use with caution.
F - Too unreliable to publish.

Source: Karen Mihorean, "Trends in Self-Reported Spousal Violence," in Kathy Au Coin, ed., *Family Violence in Canada: A Statistical Profile 2005* (Ottawa: Minister of Industry, Statistics Canada, Canadian Centre for Justice Statistics, 2005), 27.

percent of all cases the police came to the scene, and in 76 percent of cases the police made a report or conducted an investigation.

The police were most likely to give the abuser a warning or remove the abuser from the home than make an arrest or lay charges against the abuser. However, there are interesting gender differences in the police response to spousal violence as reported by the victims. Forty-eight percent of the partners of women victims were removed from the home, while this was true in 32 percent of cases for men's partners. In addition, an arrest was made or charges were laid in 41 percent of cases of spousal assault against women, while an arrest was made or charges were laid in 21 percent of cases of spousal assault against men.

THINKING ABOUT SPOUSAL VIOLENCE

The importance of disaggregating the data are once again reinforced to reveal patterned, largely gendered, victimizations. Beyond the simple statistical rate is a wealth of data that highlight the subordinate position of women in many spousal relationships, which account for greater and more serious violence at the hands of their partners. While the role of age has emerged, we know little of the dynamics in same-sex relationships or the influence of racialization on the nature and patterns of spousal assault.[1]

One ironic and perhaps telling conclusion from the data is that, in spite of decades of pouring resources into a criminal justice response to spousal violence, few men and women choose to go this route. Indeed, police are rarely called while other non-criminal justice resource, formal and informal, play a far greater role in victims' choices in the aftermath of spousal violence.

FAMILY VIOLENCE AGAINST CHILDREN AND YOUTH

As noted earlier, the General Social Survey includes victimizations of the adult population who are 15 years of age or older.[2] Consequently, it isn't possible to assess victimization rates for children or youth using this tool. Data from other sources, such as the police and child welfare agencies, must generally be relied on. In this case, the most consistently collected and disseminated sources are police-reported data, such as the revised Uniform Crime Reports (UCR2). The limitations of this source of data have been outlined in Chapter 3. To summarize, children themselves underreport abuse due to lack of knowledge that what they experienced is abuse or criminal, fear of the abuser, or lack of access to a trusted authority. Indeed, the data from the 2004 General Social Survey indicate that the youngest respondents (i.e., those between 15–17 years of age) are the least likely to report their victimization to the police (Beattie, 2005). In addition, the age at which a child is defined in child welfare legislation varies across the country, creating inconsistencies in the data. Despite the legal obligation on the part of teachers and other professionals to report suspected child abuse, a significant number of incidents likely go undetected and unreported. And, as is the case in general, police statistics do not include emotional abuse or the extent to which children witness violence (Au Coin, 2003). The data presented below are based on police-reported data for 2003 (Beattie, 2005). These data represent 122 police services across Canada and 61 percent of the total volume of crime in Canada, so they must therefore be interpreted with caution.

At the time of data collection in 2003, children and youth under 18 years of age constituted 21 percent of the Canadian population and 25 percent of victims of police-reported physical and sexual assaults (Beattie, 2005). Children and youth constituted 21 percent of victims of physical assaults and 61 percent of sexual assaults. In fact, female children and youth constituted 80 percent of victims of sexual assault. For both female and male children and youth combined, the majority of all assaults were committed by friends and/or acquaintances (at 48 percent). (See Table 5.3)

Girls were more likely to be assaulted by a family member (at 28 percent) than were boys (at 16 percent). However, boys were more likely to be assaulted by a stranger (at 22 percent) than were girls (at 14 percent). In addition, however, the proportion of assaults committed against children and youth by a family member decreased with age, while the proportion of such assaults committed by a stranger increased. Youth between the ages of 12–17 years were most likely to be assaulted by an acquaintance, followed by a stranger, and least frequently by a family member. (See Table 5.4)

When looking specifically at victimizations within the family, police-reported data indicate gender differences for sexual and physical assaults. For example, girls between the ages of 12–14 years were most at risk of sexual assaults by a family member, with the highest risk for 14-year-old

Table 5.3: Relationship of Victim and Accused in Physical and Sexual Assaults against Children and Youth, by Age

Relationship of accused to victim	Sexual Assault[1]							Physical Assault[2]						
				Age of Victim							Age of Victim			
	Total	<3	3–5	6–8	9–11	12–14	15–17	Total	<3	3–5	6–8	9–11	12–14	15–17
Total assault victims	9,352	155	1,106	1,282	1,566	2,963	2,280	27,953	560	825	1,641	3,586	9,185	12,156
	No.			No.				No.			No.			
				%							%			
Family[3]	3,020	55	49	45	40	25	19	5,828	65	62	43	23	16	16
Friend/acquaintance[4]	4,448	34	38	38	43	55	52	14,078	15	21	35	52	56	51
Stranger	1,202	4	4	9	11	14	20	5,350	8	8	12	15	19	23
Unknown[5]	682	7	9	7	6	6	9	2,697	12	9	10	9	9	10

1 - Sexual assault includes sexual assault, sexual assault with a weapon, aggravated sexual assault, and the "other sexual crimes" category, which includes sexual interference, sexual touching, sexual exploitation, incest, etc.
2 - Physical assault includes assault levels 1, 2, and 3, unlawfully causing bodily harm, discharge firearm with intent, criminal negligence causing bodily harm, and other assaults.
3 - Includes spouse, ex-spouse, parent, child, sibling, and extended family.
4 - includes any relationship in which the accused and the victim are familiar with each other, but are not related, or in a legal guardianship relationship.
5 - Includes cases where the relationship between the victim and the accused is unknown.

Source: Karen Beattie, "Family Violence against Children and Youth," in Kathy Au Coin, ed., *Family Violence in Canada: A Statistical Profile 2005* (Ottawa: Minister of Industry, Statistics Canada, Canadian Centre for Justice Statistics, 2005), 76.

Table 5.4: Age of Victim and Type of Assault against Children and Youth, by Family Members

Relationship of accused to victim	Sexual Assault[1]							Physical Assault[2]						
	Age of Victim							Age of Victim						
	Total	<3	3–5	6–8	9–11	12–14	15–17	Total	<3	3–5	6–8	9–11	12–14	15–17
Total victims	3,020	86	547	582	627	750	428	5,828	365	510	709	827	1,497	1,920
	No.							No.						
				%							%			
				No.							No.			
Parent[3]	1,213	64	44	30	33	42	52	4,057	91	84	81	77	72	53
Sibling[4]	937	19	30	39	35	30	20	1,030	4	9	11	15	20	25
Extended Family[5]	844	17	25	31	32	27	25	452	5	7	9	8	6	9
Spouse/ex-spouse[6]	26	0	0	0	0	2	3	289	0	0	0	0	2	13

1 - Sexual assault includes sexual assault, sexual assault with a weapon, aggravated sexual assault, and the "other sexual crimes" category, which includes sexual interference, sexual touching, sexual exploitation, incest, etc.

2 - Physical assault includes assault levels 1, 2, and 3, unlawfully causing bodily harm, discharge firearm with intent, criminal negligence causing bodily harm, and other assaults.

3 - Includes a small number of cases where age or the relationship between the accused and the victim may have been miscoded.

4 - Sibling includes natural, step, half, foster, or adopted siblings.

5 - Extended family includes others related by blood, marriage, adoption, or foster care.

6 - Spouses/ex-spouses include legally married, common-law, separated, and divorced partners.

Source: Karen Beattie, "Family Violence against Children and Youth," in Kathy Au Coin, ed., *Family Violence in Canada: A Statistical Profile 2005* (Ottawa: Minister of Industry, Statistics Canada, Canadian Centre for Justice Statistics, 2005).

girls (at 160 per 100,000). The greatest risk for sexual assault for boys was between 4 to 6 years old, with the highest risk for 4-year-olds (at 54 per 100,000). With respect to physical assaults against children under the age of 12, boys were at greatest risk. However, girls were the most at risk for children and youth between the ages of 13–17 years of age.

There were also important patterns with respect to the family members who were most likely to be accused of physical and sexual assaults within the family. For example, parents accounted for 70 percent of family members accused of physical assaults against children and youth and 40 percent of family members accused of sexual assaults against children and youth. Parents were more likely to be the accused in physical assaults for both girls and boys.

The influence of gender is also evident when looking at the accused in physical and sexual assaults within the family that were reported to the police. Seventy-two percent of the accused in cases of physical assaults against all family members reported to the police were men: 61 percent were fathers, 21 percent were brothers, 8 percent were extended family members, and 10 percent were spouses. Ninety-eight percent of the accused in cases of sexual assaults against all family members reported to the police were men: 38 percent were fathers, 33 percent were brothers, and 28 percent were male extended family members.

THINKING ABOUT FAMILY VIOLENCE AGAINST CHILDREN AND YOUTH

We begin to see, through the data presented above, the pervasive nature of violence in the lives of children and youth, both for female and male children. This violence is overwhelmingly perpetrated in the earliest years by those closest to them. While the gendered nature of this abuse has been clearly shown, the abusers of young are overwhelming men, who are mostly fathers, but also brothers, uncles, and trusted family friends. As children mature, they face the additional threat of acquaintances and strangers at a rate that outstrips those of adults. This is perhaps the best, if tragic, case for looking closely at a social world and cultural context that permits children to be so utterly exploited by those who care for them.

FAMILY VIOLENCE AGAINST OLDER ADULTS

In spite of the range of methodologies available to measure victimization, Au Coin (2003) notes that difficulties in uncovering abuse of the elderly remain. There are similar concerns facing many victims (e.g., fear of retaliation, lack of knowledge that what they are experiencing is, in fact, criminal). In addition, however, the increasing dependency of many elderly people puts them at increased risk for abuse by family members, caregivers, institutional staff, as well as strangers. These factors may also create barriers to reporting or accessing other services. At the same time, detecting abuse among the elderly may be difficult due to the more limited access they often have to the community, whether they are living in residential or institutional settings.

Limited self-reported victimization data on elder abuse within the family are available as part of the 1999 General Social Survey (Pottie Bunge and Locke, 2000).[3] The sample included respondents aged 65 years and older who were asked a range of questions about emotional, financial, and physical abuse they may have experienced at the hands of children, caregivers, and spouses. It is important to keep in mind that the General Social Survey excludes individuals living in institutions. While the percentage of older adults living in institutions is fairly small, they would likely include those at greatest risk. In addition, "telephone surveys are expected to undercount incidents of abuse directed at victims who are confined to their rooms without access to telephones, or who are isolated in some other manner" (Pottie Bunge and Locke, 2000, p. 27). The data therefore likely underestimate the rates of abuse against older adults living in institutions, and those who do not speak English or French.

Approximately 1 percent of respondents in the 1999 General Social Survey reported being physically or sexually assaulted by a spouse, adult child, or caregiver (Pottie Bunge and Locke, 2000). Seven percent of elderly respondents reported some sort of emotional or financial abuse, mostly by spouses. Emotional abuse (at 7 percent) was more commonly reported than financial abuse (at 1 percent). The most frequently reported type of abuse included being put down or called names, and limiting contact with family or friends. Virtually all of this abuse was committed by spouses.

Pottie Bunge and Locke (2000) state that "[o]lder adults from all income brackets, education levels and age groups reported some form of emotional or financial abuse" (p. 28). At the same time, men (at 9 percent) reported more emotional or financial abuse than women (at 6 percent) as did older adults who were divorced or separated (at 13 percent). With respect to household income, emotional and financial abuse was highest for those whose income was between $30,000 and $39,999 and those whose household income was more than $60,000, at 11 percent for each group. Older adults with some post-secondary education reported higher levels of abuse (at 9 percent) than those with other levels of education, such as a high-school diploma (at 6 percent) or a university degree (at 8 percent).

Limitations of police-reported data notwithstanding, they provide information on the nature of family violence against the elderly that comes to the attention of the police (Au Coin, 2005a). Overall, those 65 years of age and older are the least likely to come to the attention of the police as victims of violent crime. Of those who do, 46 percent of this group were women, and 54 percent were men. Fifty-four percent of women victims were victimized by someone outside the family, while this was the case for 71 percent of men. (See Table 5.5)

The police-reported data indicate that older female victims are more likely to be victimized by someone within the family (at 39 percent), most likely a spouse or an adult child. Twenty percent of men are victimized by someone within the family, most frequently by an adult child or by a spouse. When a family member was the perpetrator, the most frequent type of victimization was common assault, followed by uttering threats. (See Table 5.6) This pattern held for both female and male victims. When the perpetrator was a non-family member, the most common type of victimization was also assault, although it was followed in frequency by robbery. Again, this pattern held for both female and male victims.

Similar findings emerge with respect to family abuse against the elderly as was found in family violence against children: the vast majority of the accused (78 percent) in such cases were male family members (Au Coin, 2005a). When the victim was an older female, the proportion of male accused increased to 85 percent, including spouses or former spouses (at 43 percent) and sons (at 30 percent). This is in contrast to the case of older men, where the accused is a son (in 39 percent of cases), followed by a spouse or former spouse (in 31 percent of cases). Ten percent of female accused were a current or former spouse, 6 percent were daughters, and 6 percent were extended family members.

THINKING ABOUT FAMILY VIOLENCE AGAINST OLDER ADULTS

The elderly constitute a very small proportion of victims of crime, whether measured by victimization surveys or police-reported data. While

Table 5.5: Number and Proportion of Older Adult Victims of Crime, by Sex and Relationship of Accused

| Relationship of accused to victim | Total | | Sex of Victim | | | |
| | | | Female | | Male | |
	No.	%	No.	%	No.	%
Total violence against older adults	**3,978**	**100**	**1,830**	**100**	**2,148**	**100**
Total family	**1,141**	**29**	**714**	**39**	**427**	**20**
Current spouse[1]	326	8	240	13	86	4
Ex-spouse	46	1	22	1	24	1
Parent	89	2	45	2	44	2
Adult child	380	10	237	13	143	7
Sibling[2]	151	4	94	5	57	3
Extended family[3]	149	4	76	4	73	3
Total non-family	**2,504**	**63**	**987**	**54**	**1,517**	**71**
Close friend	205	5	84	5	121	6
Business relationship	202	5	57	3	145	7
Casual acquaintance	763	19	283	15	480	22
Stranger	1,334	34	563	31	771	36
Unknown[4]	**333**	**8**	**129**	**7**	**204**	**9**

1 – "Current spouse" includes legally married and common-law partners.
2 – "Sibling" includes natural, step, half, foster, or adopted brother or sister.
3 – "Extended family" includes all others related to the victim either by blood or by marriage, e.g., aunts, uncles, cousins, and in-laws.
4 – "Unknown" includes cases where the relationship between the victim and the accused is unknown.

Source: Kathy Au Coin, "Family Violence against Older Adults," in Kathy Au Coin, ed., *Family Violence in Canada: A Statistical Profile 2005* (Ottawa: Minister of Industry, Statistics Canada, Canadian Centre for Justice Statistics, 2005), 82.

Table 5.6: Number and Proportion of Older Adult Victims, by Type of Crime and Relationship to Accused

Type of violent crime	Offences Committed by Family						Offences Committed by Non-Family					
	Total		Sex of Victim				Total		Sex of Victim			
			Female		Male				Female		Male	
	No.	%	No.	%	No.	%	No.	%	No.	%	No.	%
Total violent offences	**1,141**	**100**	**714**	**100**	**427**	**100**	**2,504**	**100**	**987**	**100**	**1,517**	**100**
Sexual assault	6	1	6	1	0	0	71	3	66	7	5	0
Major assault (assault levels 2 & 3)	180	16	95	13	85	20	274	11	72	7	202	13
Common assault (assault level 1)	628	55	409	57	219	51	814	33	261	26	553	36
Robbery	11	1	6	1	5	1	692	28	349	35	343	23
Criminal harassment	49	4	34	5	15	4	127	5	71	7	56	4
Uttering threats	221	19	137	19	84	20	434	17	133	13	301	20
Other violent offences[1]	46	4	27	4	19	4	92	4	35	4	57	4

1 – "Other violent offences" include unlawfully causing bodily harm, criminal negligence causing bodily harm, other assaults, kidnapping, extortion, hostage-taking, explosives causing death/bodily harm, arson, and other violent violations.

Source: Kathy Au Coin, "Family Violence against Older Adults," in Kathy Au Coin, ed., *Family Violence in Canada: A Statistical Profile 2005* (Ottawa: Minister of Industry, Statistics Canada, Canadian Centre for Justice Statistics, 2005), 82.

encouraging, the extent of their overall vulnerability (physical, emotional, financial, and social) heightens and complicates their exposure and risk to victimization and exploitation. What is also troubling is that the patterns of exploitation by those closest to them extends to this stage in their lives, and is the most pronounced, again, by male perpetrators. Here, however, we can add male children into the equation, along with current and former spouses, brothers, and brothers-in-law. The inescapable conclusion is that risk of victimization, too often identified as a characteristic of victims or their day-to-day activities, must also be seen as closely aligned with men and masculinity, which extends from the earliest stages of childhood into the later years.

NOTES

1. The nature and patterns of spousal violence against Aboriginal victims is discussed in Chapter 6.
2. Participants in the General Social Survey were required to be at least 16 years of age. However, since some of the questions referred to the time period within the last 12 months, estimates of victimization could be made for those as young as 15 years of age.
3. Data on victimization of older Canadians as part of the 2004 General Social Survey were not available at the time this manuscript was prepared.

QUESTIONS FOR FURTHER CONSIDERATION

1. Can you identify themes across all forms of family violence (spousal violence, violence against children and youth, and abuse of older adults) that emerge from the data? How might you understand them?
2. Given what we know about the patterns of violence within the family, how effective do you think the criminal law would be in responding to this type of crime? Identify and discuss both the strengths and weaknesses of a criminal law response.

CHAPTER 6

Challenging Victimizations: Two Cases in Point

IN OUR EARLIER discussions on defining "victim" (see Chapter 2), we noted that a serious limitation to most definitions is that they fail to give sufficient attention to systemic forms of victimization. That is, we tend not to include those victimizations that cannot be seen as random, isolated acts between strangers but as reflective of social inequities that pervade the lives of many, such as people of colour, religious and sexual minorities, and women. This concern applies to the identification, designation, and measurement of "victim." Two cases are used to make this point. First, we look at the overrepresentation of Aboriginal peoples as victims of crime. While there is no shortage of criminal justice data to confirm this, their overrepresentation extends throughout the criminal justice system to economic, educational, and social arenas (Brzozowski et al., 2006). A singular focus on criminal victimization cleanses the experiences of Aboriginal peoples from the broader context in a misleading way. Below we present data that are indicative of the deeper roots of colonialism, dislocation, and neglect experienced by Aboriginal peoples at the hands of Canadian authorities over time.

The second case concerns the limitations of relying almost exclusively on the criminal law to respond to hate "crimes" in Canada. Hate crime legislation, while valuable, is an attempt to define and measure as "crime" incidents that are both systemic in nature and pervasive throughout Canadian society. Neither the criminal law nor the tools we use to measure victimization are equipped to respond to hate-motivated activity in other social institutions or in the community more broadly defined. Like the violence experienced by Aboriginal peoples, hate crimes are not isolated incidents against isolated victims, are problematically defined, and are inadequately measured.

ABORIGINAL PEOPLES, VICTIMIZATION, AND THE CRIMINAL PROCESS

Perhaps one of the most persistent findings in Canadian criminal justice is that Aboriginal peoples in Canada are vastly overrepresented in the criminal justice process compared to their representation in the population as a whole. This is true with respect to Aboriginal peoples both as victims and offenders. The 2004 General Social Survey indicated that Aboriginal peoples were at generally higher risk of criminal victimization, violent victimization, and multiple victimizations than was the non-Aboriginal population (Brzozowski et al., 2006). (See Figure 6.1)

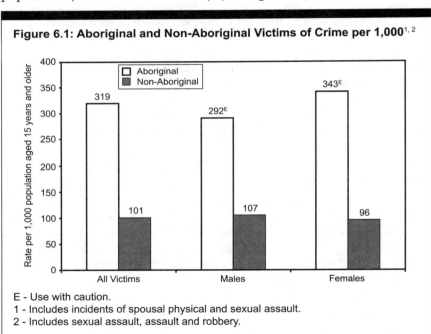

Figure 6.1: Aboriginal and Non-Aboriginal Victims of Crime per 1,000[1,2]

E - Use with caution.
1 - Includes incidents of spousal physical and sexual assault.
2 - Includes sexual assault, assault and robbery.

Source: Jodi-Ann Brzozowski, Andrea Taylor-Butts, and Sarah Johnson, "Victimization and Offending Among the Aboriginal Population in Canada," *Juristat* 26(3) (2006): 5.

Indeed, twice as many Aboriginal peoples as non-Aboriginal people reported being victimized two or more times in the preceding 12 months. As with the non-Aboriginal population, those between 15–24 years of age are at greatest risk of victimization. Compared to the non-Aboriginal population, Aboriginal peoples are more likely to know the perpetrator, and the incidents are more likely to occur in the victim's home. At the extreme levels of violence, we find that Aboriginal peoples are almost nine times more likely to be killed than are non-Aboriginal people; this rate is even higher for Aboriginal males.

According to the 2004 General Social Survey (Mihorean, 2005a), higher rates of Aboriginal victimization also emerged in the context of spousal assaults. Twenty-one percent of Aboriginal respondents reported being victims of spousal violence, three times the frequency reported by non-Aboriginal people. (See Figure 6.2) There was no statistical difference

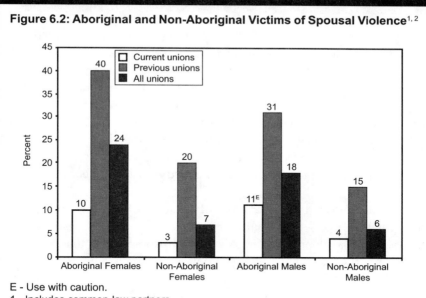

Figure 6.2: Aboriginal and Non-Aboriginal Victims of Spousal Violence[1,2]

E - Use with caution.
1 - Includes common-law partners.
2 - Excludes people who refused to state their marital status.

Source: Jodi-Ann Brzozowski, Andrea Taylor-Butts, and Sarah Johnson. "Victimization and Offending Among the Aboriginal Population in Canada," *Juristat* 26(3) (2006): 7.

between Aboriginal women (at 24 percent) and Aboriginal men (at 18 percent) in reporting. However, Aboriginal respondents reported experiencing more serious violence on the part of their spouses: 41 percent reported being either beaten, choked, threatened with a gun or knife, had a gun or knife used against them, or were sexually assaulted. This was the case for 27 percent of non-Aboriginal respondents. Indeed, 43 percent of Aboriginal respondents (versus 31 percent of non-Aboriginal respondents) reported injury as a result of the spousal violence, and 33 percent of Aboriginal respondents (versus 22 percent of non-Aboriginal respondents) stated that they feared for their lives as a result of the spousal violence they experienced. Aboriginal women and men reported higher rates of emotional abuse by a current or former partner (at 36 percent) than did non-Aboriginal women and men (at 17 percent).

It is important to point out at this time that the General Social Survey, with all its methodological strengths, nevertheless systematically excludes significant segments of Aboriginal communities across Canada. For example, the exclusion of the Yukon, Northwest Territories, and Nunavut in the 1999 version, and their inclusion in the 2004 version as only a pilot is, from the outset, highly prejudicial to Aboriginal populations across Canada. In addition, conducting interviews over the phone, and only in English and French, would likely screen out many Aboriginal peoples who do not have phones or cannot speak either one of these languages with sufficient fluency to complete the interview. This would affect not just those living in territorial communities, but many living on reserves, as well as the many off-reserve, marginalized Aboriginal peoples living in urban centres.

In spite of data that indicate a higher level of victimization among Aboriginal peoples, these data nevertheless likely underestimate the extent of the problem among Aboriginal peoples in Canada. This is particularly the case when relying on police-level data, where information on the identity victims is often not collected or classified as "unknown" (Brzozowski et al., 2006). In addition, however, many have noted that there is not always a clear distinction between "victim" and "non-victim" (Comack, 2006; Stanko, 1995), or even "victim" and "offender" (Rock, 1994), which a narrow focus on victimization often overlooks. In the context of the lives of Aboriginal peoples, it is critical to see victimization in the broader context of conflict with the administration of justice and not narrowly linked to victim status. We see from the data that Aboriginal peoples have more dealings with the police, courts, and correctional components of the criminal justice system, which itself is linked with other forms of social inequality.

For example, at the earliest stages, differences between Aboriginal and non-Aboriginal populations emerge in the nature and extent of contact with the police. Based on data from the 2004 General Social Survey (Brzozowski et al., 2006), Aboriginal peoples were more likely to come in contact with the police as victims of crime (13 percent vs. 7 percent for the non-Aboriginal population), as witnesses to crime (11 percent vs. 6 percent for the non-Aboriginal population), and for being arrested (5 percent vs. 1 percent for the non-Aboriginal population). Perhaps not surprisingly, Aboriginal respondents were less likely to rate the police as doing a good job in a variety of contexts: 50 percent stated the police were doing a good job at ensuring the safety of citizens (vs. 62 percent of non-Aboriginal respondents), 48 percent stated the police were doing a good job at enforcing laws (vs. 60 percent of non-Aboriginal respondents), and 45 percent stated the police were doing a good job at responding to calls promptly (vs. 52 percent of non-Aboriginal respondents) (Brzozowski et al., 2006).

This higher level of contact with the criminal justice system extends to the degree to which Aboriginal peoples are represented in custodial facilities. In 2003/2004, Aboriginal peoples constituted 2.6 percent of the population of Canada. However, they constituted 18 percent of admissions to federal custody, 21 percent of admissions to provincial/territorial sentenced custody, 19 percent of admissions to conditional sentences, 18 percent of admissions to remand, and 16 percent of admissions to probation. As Brzozowski et al. (2006) note, in the 10-year period between 1994/1995 and 2003/2004, the proportion of Aboriginal adult admissions to custody has increased, while Aboriginal adult admissions to community supervision (i.e., probation, conditional sentences) have remained stable. Aboriginal inmates were characteristic in that they were younger, had less education, and were more likely to be unemployed than non-Aboriginal inmates (Brzozowski et al., 2006). They have also been assessed to have higher needs than non-Aboriginal inmates, particularly in the areas of substance abuse, personal needs, employment and family/marital needs, and were considered to be at higher risk for reoffending (Finn et al., 1999).

In the context of Aboriginal youth, they constitute 5 percent of the population in Canada, but 21 percent of admissions to open custody, 20 percent of admissions to secure custody, 19 percent of admissions to deferred custody, and 12 percent of admissions to probation. While admission of Aboriginal youth to custody had been declining in the 10 years preceding the implementation of the *Youth Criminal Justice Act* in 2002/2003, the *proportion* of Aboriginal youth admitted to sentenced custody and remand began showing a sharp increase at that time (Brzozowski et al., 2006). More specifically, between 2002/2003 and 2003/2004 the number of Aboriginal youth sentenced to custody decreased by 33 percent, but the number of non-Aboriginal youth sentenced to custody decreased by 51 percent. For admissions to remand, there was a 3 percent increase in Aboriginal youth, but a 17 percent decrease in admissions of non-Aboriginal youth.

THE SOCIAL CONTEXT OF ABORIGINAL PEOPLES AND THE CRIMINAL JUSTICE SYSTEM

We begin to see how these findings need to be placed within the historical, political, economic, and social context of Aboriginal peoples in Canada.

> We do not believe, for instance, that there is anything about Aboriginal people or their culture that predisposes them to criminal behaviour. Instead, we believe that the causes of Aboriginal criminal behaviour are rooted in a long history of discrimination and social inequality that has impoverished Aboriginal people and consigned them to the margins of Manitoban society. (Aboriginal Justice Inquiry of Manitoba, 1991, p. 85)

This statement receives support from findings with respect to the broader social and economic location of Aboriginal peoples in Canada.

For example, according to the 1996 Census, almost 230,000 Aboriginal people (either North American Indian, Métis, or Inuit) lived on reserves across Canada, and almost 50 percent of the Aboriginal population lived in communities classified as rural (Canadian Centre for Justice Statistics,

Box 6.1: Wounds Run Deep on Remote Reserves
Kashechewan Tip of Iceberg
Ailments Point to Larger Social Ills
by Trish Crawford, Life writer

The children were suffering.

Leo Friday, chief of the Kashechewan Reserve—where the water has been so contaminated with E. coli and sediment that residents have been boiling drinking water for most of the past decade—says the related skin rashes and infections were hardest on the little ones.

"There were a lot of problems with the kids. If they had a wound, a sore, it would not heal."

One desperate father begged for airfare to send his child to Timmins to treat the oozing mouth sores that so distorted the boy's looks that children at school were teasing him. Eventually, the 9-year-old was healed by a battery of powerful medicines.

"The father almost cried," the chief said. "He sees that his son is beginning to heal."

Another child with horrible scabies was also flown out for treatment and Friday's own granddaughter has a persistent sore on her cheek that won't close over.

That's why Friday ultimately declared a state of emergency and turned to the province for help with the physical and psychological ills plaguing his beleaguered community of 1,700 residents on the coast of James Bay.

Federal government neglect, lack of resources, substandard living conditions and a fragmented delivery of health services all contributed to Kashechewan's problems, native leaders say.

And a public health specialist who treats Toronto's native community and has served extensively in the north, agrees.

Dr. Chandrakant Shah says the residents of Kashechewan were particularly vulnerable to the effects of water contamination, which can range from diarrhea and fever to Hepatitis A.

Mostly, people infected with E. coli feel run down and without energy, he says. The most vulnerable are the elderly, those with compromised immune systems, and children, he says.

A total of 30 per cent of Kashechewan's population is under the age of 14.

Asthma is also widespread in the community and Shah says those using steroids, which can weaken the immune system, would also be more affected.

As a community, Kashechewan was particularly vulnerable to water illnesses because as many as 17 people can share a house. It's difficult to boil water for baths, so hygiene suffers and skin ailments flourish—jumping from person to person in close quarters, he explains.

"What is happening is that the water is just a symptom of something larger—the larger problems of many First Nations communities," he says.

The social determinants of health such as housing, employment and income are lacking on reserves. He is particularly irked by the high food prices natives must pay in remote communities, limiting access to good nutrition.

A bottle of beer or wine costs the same in Toronto as it does in Timmins, Shah says. But the same is not true of food. This means spirits in the north are subsidized but food is not, he says.

Most of the children have now been evacuated from the Kashechewan community. There, you'll find fetid water sitting in ditches and the smell of oil wafting from ponds.

The dump is located near the water intake system. According to Chief Friday, the original estimated price tag for the water treatment plant was $19 million. But, in the end, the federal government paid just $2.5 million, far less than required, he says.

And sediment has repeatedly been found in the drinking water, according to an official with Indian Affairs. That official told the Star the federal government has been tinkering with the Kashechewan water system for years. After flooding and breakdowns, it has been closed in the past, and occasionally residents have been given bottled water.

But for 10 years, on and off, residents have been boiling their drinking water—a laborious process because so many must chop wood virtually non-stop to keep stoves going. They have been collecting rainwater from their roofs for showers as the heavily chlorinated tap water causes or exacerbates rampant skin infections such as impetigo.

The current fragmented health delivery system caused some of Kashechewan's problems as no one group took full responsibility, says Pat Chilton, CEO of the local Weeneebayko Health Authority.

"There are three different jurisdictions and three different ways of dealing with communities," Chilton says.

What happened in Kashechewan "was neglect, pure and simple," he says.

The three agencies involved in addressing the natives' health-care needs were the federal government, the provincial government and the Weeneebayko Health Authority. All had different responsibilities.

Normal medicines administered by federal government nurses couldn't keep the skin ailments under control, Friday says.

Doctors visited the reserve from Moose Factory, on James Bay, from the health authority. There, for $32 million a year, it runs a hospital providing doctors, dentists and diabetes programs to surrounding reserves. It operates as an independent authority and gets money from the federal government.

This fragmented health system also includes provincially-run hospitals and services in the James Bay area.

Friday would have liked a small hospital on the reserve.

A unified Aboriginal health service to coordinate and deliver health programs to all of the First Nations people, jointly funded by the Ontario and federal government, is scheduled to start next year. It has been on the books since 1989, says Chilton.

But, unfortunately, water isn't the only health problem and Kashechewan isn't the only reserve that is suffering.

A number of chiefs, who sit on the Weeneebayko board and attended this week's Ontario Hospital Association convention in Toronto, told the Star their communities are also experiencing severe health problems.

There are 50 reserves currently under boil water orders, says Mike Metatawabin, chief at Fort Albany on James Bay.

Because native affairs is a federal responsibility, there is a widely-held belief that the Canadian government is taking care of them properly and there is no role for other levels of government, he says. This, he says, results in second-class services.

Metatawabin says provincial government standards on health issues—especially for drinking water—are higher than the federal government's and, as citizens of Ontario, they deserve the same treatment as other Ontarians.

Public attitudes towards First Nations people will only change if their history and culture is included in the Ontario school curriculum, says Metatawabin. He added this could ensure there is the will and resources to address their problems.

Patricia Akiwenzie, chief of Moose Cree, just south of James Bay, says poor housing and overcrowding on reserves is hurting the children's development, in education and in health, for example.

"It is like a stunt on the child," she says. "A child is sharing one room with father and mother and sibling. Where is the opportunity to do homework? How can they grow—they need space. Instead, they are stunted."

Poor housing affects health in other ways, she says. There are cases where mould is causing rampant asthma and substandard wooden panelling is a fire hazard, she says.

She is interested in setting up a native-run store on her reserve, complaining that there is price gouging by the northern stores, which have long sold food and hard goods to natives in a near monopoly. Cheap, healthy food should be available on reserves, she says.

The illness and poverty on reserves "is Canada's shame," she says.

Mike Carpenter, chief of Attawapiskat, south of James Bay, complains that the school on his reserve had to be closed in 2000, due to soil contamination. This is the legacy of an oil pipe that ruptured on the reserve in the 1970s, spilling 38,000 gallons of fuel into the ground, he says.

The students are still in portables and the soil has not been cleaned up yet, Carpenter says, adding that people on the reserve felt some local cancers were connected to the contamination.

"People are sick," Carpenter says. His reserve also has a boil water order.

Lack of funds means his reserve has no police on duty after 2 a.m., he says, adding that this has thrown their ambulance services in jeopardy as attendants fear "getting roughed up" on alcohol-related calls. In all other communities in Ontario, Carpenter points out, the ambulance attendants would receive police assistance on such cases.

"Why are First Nations treated differently than all others in Ontario?" he asks.

Nelson Wiseman, political science professor at the University of Toronto, says the situation in Kashechewan "is tragic" but that moving people 30 kilometres away (one of the possibilities currently being studied) won't solve the problem. When residents from Davis Inlet were relocated to another remote community in February 2002 to address an epidemic of solvent addiction, the isolation and unemployment continued to result in addiction and depression, he says.

He speculated that some of the Kashechewan residents would not go back, especially if they find work in the North Bay and Sudbury areas where they have been relocated. Many of the residents of New Orleans who were evacuated after hurricane Katrina have successfully settled in their new communities, Wiseman says.

He argues that possibly the isolated reserve should be abandoned for the sake of everyone's health, adding that these are not traditional living areas for many. (For example, chief Friday says the settlement at Kashechewan is less than 50 years old.)

"The problem in Kashechewan is not just water," Wiseman says. "Virtually everyone is unemployed."

Any solution must come from the native people themselves, Wiseman says.

"It is not for us to decide."

When Walkerton's contaminated water system came to light in 2000, bottled water was quickly provided for extended periods of time, there was a public outcry and the water system was fixed, Shah says. But Kashechewan has been boiling its water for a decade and nobody cared, he says.

"If it was a white community, it would have been different."

Source: Trish Crawford, "Wounds Run Deep on Remote Reserves, Kashechewan Tip of Iceberg," *Toronto Star* (November 4, 2005), D01.

2001). Only 25 percent of Aboriginal people lived in urban communities. In contrast, roughly 75 percent of the non-Aboriginal population lived in urban communities at the time of the census. The Aboriginal population was, on average, 10 years younger than the general population, at 25.5 years. Aboriginal seniors constituted 4 percent of the Aboriginal population, while seniors constituted 12 percent of the non-Aboriginal population.

At all age levels, Aboriginal peoples were less likely to be attending school than were non-Aboriginal people: 68 percent of Aboriginal peoples aged 15–19 were attending school (either full-time or part-time), while 83 percent of non-Aboriginal peoples in the same age group were attending school. Fifty-four percent of Aboriginal peoples had not completed high school compared with 34 percent of the non-Aboriginal population. Three percent of Aboriginal peoples aged 15 years and older had a university degree compared to 13 percent of the non-Aboriginal population.

At the time of the 1996 Census, Aboriginal peoples were underemployed in a number of ways. Just under half of Aboriginal men were in the paid workforce, while 41 percent of Aboriginal women were in the paid workforce. This is compared to 66 percent of non-Aboriginal men and 53 percent of non-Aboriginal women who were in the paid workforce, respectively. Twenty-four percent of the Aboriginal labour force was unemployed (i.e., "not working for pay or profit, but who are looking for employment") (Canadian Centre for Justice Statistics, 2001, note 9), while only 10 percent of the non-Aboriginal labour force was unemployed. These rates were highest for Aboriginal labour force participants between the ages of 15–24 years, particularly males. At the same time, employed Aboriginal peoples tended to have jobs in low-paying occupations, while they were underrepresented in management positions and professional occupations. Given the larger context of low education levels and underemployment, it is not surprising that the incomes of Aboriginal peoples are also lower: in 1995, Aboriginal peoples had an average income that was 62 percent of that of the non-Aboriginal population, at $15,700.

> Low incomes, unemployment, poor health care, inadequate levels of education, crowded and substandard housing conditions—all are characteristics of Aboriginal life in Canada. It is crucial to recognize that the social condition of Aboriginal people is a direct result of the discriminatory and repressive policies that successive European and Canadian governments have directed towards Aboriginal people. (Aboriginal Justice Inquiry of Manitoba, 1991, p. 92)

Monture-Angus (1999) and others (Comack and Balfour, 2004; Razack, 2000; Samuelson and Monture-Angus, 2002) make the direct link between criminal justice, racism, and colonial practices, all of which must be confronted to understand and alleviate structural inequality for Aboriginal peoples. This cannot be done by isolating the institution of criminal justice from other arenas.

> Although recognition of the need for appropriate justice services must underpin attempts to overcome the imposition of what is essentially a foreign mode of criminal justice, that approach alone will not ensure a different future. The severe problems, after all, arise as a direct consequence of colonialism. A recognition of the colonial underpinnings of the justice — and injustice — system must provide the basic context for any efforts at substantial change. (Samuelson and Monture-Angus, 2002, p. 169)

HATE CRIMES IN CANADA

> The Jews damn near owned all of Germany prior to the war. That's how Hitler came in. He was going to make damn sure that the Jews didn't take over Germany or Europe. That's why he fried six million of those guys, you know. Jews would have owned the God-damned world. And look what they're doing. They're killing people in Arab countries. (Cook, 2005, p. A20)

These comments were made in December 2002 by David Ahenakew, former head of the Assembly of First Nations and a recipient of the Order of Canada, to a reporter after a speech to the Federation of Saskatchewan Indian Nations. His comments shocked both the Jewish and Aboriginal communities, and sparked considerable debate about the most appropriate official response. His comments were clearly anti-Semitic and hateful, but were they "criminal"? If they were indeed found to be criminal, would the imposition of criminal sanctions be sufficient on their own to bring home to Ahenakew and others like him the seriousness of making such statements publicly?

Ahenakew was eventually charged and convicted of promoting hatred against an identifiable group under section 319(1) of the *Criminal Code of*

Canada and fined $1,000. In addition, however, the federal government revoked his Order of Canada, and he was condemned by many within his own community despite being an accomplished leader and advocate for the rights of Aboriginal peoples in Canada. Nevertheless, at a press conference held immediately after his conviction, he remained unrepentant, blaming the "Jewish lobby" for his conviction at trial and losing his Order of Canada (Harding, 2005). In June 2005, Ahenakew's conviction was overturned by the Court of Appeal, which found that he lacked the necessary intent that the law requires to make a criminal conviction. This case clearly highlights that the criminal law is a blunt instrument for dealing with many acts and behaviours that might be considered hateful. In addition, we will see that the tools used to measure victimization are ill equipped to measure what are essentially systemic problems. This applies to both police-reported data, as well as victimization surveys. The remainder of this chapter will demonstrate both the limitations of the criminal law as a tool to define hate, as well as the limitations of the standard methodologies we use to measure it.

RESPONDING TO HATE

One of the most salient tools available in defining and responding to hate crimes in Canada is the criminal law. The substance of the *Criminal Code* provisions is outlined in Box 6.2.

We see here that hate crimes legislation tries to strike a balance between the freedom of individuals to hold negative, even hateful thoughts about individuals or groups, while placing limits on how far they may go in acting on those thoughts and feelings. The most extreme case is identified in section 318 on "Advocating Genocide," which prohibits "supporting or arguing for the killing of members of an identifiable group." This is the most serious and the rarest of criminal charges. The definition turns on the enumeration of who or which "identifiable groups" are protected by the criminal law, and requires the permission of the Attorney General of the province in order for such charges to proceed.

While the crime of advocating genocide is clearly the most serious of the *Criminal Code* offences, section 319(1) prohibits "Public Incitement of Hatred" "in such a way that there will likely be a breach of the peace" and includes communicating, in a public place, hatred against an identifiable group. Section 319(3) identifies defences to the crime. For example,

Box 6.2: Hate Crimes Provisions under the Canadian *Criminal Code*

Section 318: Advocating Genocide

The criminal act of "advocating genocide" is defined as supporting or arguing for the killing of members of an "identifiable group"—people distinguished by their colour, race, religion, or ethnic origin. The intention or motivation would be the destruction of members of the targeted group. Any person who promotes genocide is guilty of an indictable offence and liable to imprisonment for a term not exceeding five years.

Defining Genocide

Section 318 defines genocide as any acts committed with intent to destroy an identifiable group—such as killing members of the group, or deliberately inflicting conditions of life calculated to bring about the group's physical destruction.

Section 319(1): Public Incitement of Hatred

The crime of "publicly inciting hatred" has four main elements. To contravene the Code, a person must:

- communicate (by telephone, broadcasting or other audible or visible means) statements (words that may be spoken, written or recorded, gestures, and signs or other visible representations),
- in a public place (i.e., one to which the public has access by right or invitation, express or implied),
- incite hatred against an identifiable group,
- in such a way that there will likely be a breach of the peace.

All the above elements must be proven for a court to find an accused guilty of either:

- an indictable offence, for which the punishment is imprisonment for a term not exceeding two years; or
- an offence punishable on summary conviction.

Section 319(3) identifies acceptable defences. Indicates that no person shall be convicted of an offence if the statements in question:

- are established to be true
- were relevant to any subject of public interest, the discussion of which was for the public benefit, and if on reasonable grounds it was believed to be true

- were expressed in good faith, it was attempted to establish by argument and opinion on a religious subject
- were expressed in good faith, it was intended to point out, for the purpose of removal, matters tending to produce feelings of hatred toward an identifiable group in Canada

Enhanced Sentencing Provisions for Hate Crimes
The courts may define the motivations of hate, bias, or prejudice as aggravating factors when sentencing an offender for other offences, such as assault, damage to property, threatening, or harassment. The result is usually a more severe punishment (section 718.2(a)(i)).

Warrant of Seizure
Section 320 of the Criminal Code provides for the seizure and forfeiture of physical hate propaganda material kept on any premises for distribution or sale.

Source: http://www.media-awareness.ca/English/resources/legislation/canadian_law/
federal/criminal_code/criminal_code-hate.cfm

individuals have the right to hold hateful opinions and the freedom to express those thoughts under certain circumstance, such as if they are believed to be true or if expressing them is in the "public interest."

Hate provisions in the *Criminal Code* highlight a significant limitation of using the criminal law to respond to such activities: Many hate-mongers use their criminal trials to "educate" the public about ideas they believe are unpopular or suppressed and may receive more attention for their unpopular views, in addition to a platform (i.e., the criminal trial) from which to air them. In addition, the technical approach that the law takes to prove each element of the offence may derail attempts to get to the essence of hateful behaviour. This point was highlighted in the case of *R. v. Krymowski* ([2005] 1 S.C.R 101, 2005 SCC). In that case, "skinheads" protested outside a motel in Scarborough, Ontario, where a group of Roma refugees was being housed. The protesters had placards stating, among other things, "Honk If You Hate Gypsies," "Canada Is Not a Trash Can," and "G.S.T. — Gypsies Suck Tax." They also chanted "Gypsies Out," "How Do You Like Canada Now?" and "White Power." The protesters were charged with wilfully promoting hatred against an identifiable group. In the information laid against the accused, the term "Roma" appeared instead of "Gypsy" to reflect the more acceptable terminology and language preferred by the Roma themselves.

At the trial, the defence successfully argued that the terms "Roma" and "Gypsies" are not interchangeable, and therefore the accused should not be found guilty of promoting hatred against the Roma. The trial judge found that there was "no evidence whatsoever, or in any form, establishing beyond a reasonable doubt the wilful promotion of hatred against Roma or that Roma are one and the same as or also known as Gypsies." The decision was upheld at the appellate level, and went all the way to the Supreme Court of Canada for a final resolution. The Supreme Court of Canada concluded that, rather than turn on narrow definitions of "Roma" versus "Gypsies,"

> [t]he relevant questions to be asked with respect to this element of the offence were whether the Crown had proved beyond a reasonable doubt that the respondents made some or all of the statements alleged in the information and whether the statements made, as a matter of fact, promoted hatred of the Roma.

In doing so, the Court ruled, the trial judge should have looked at the totality of the evidence: (1) the motel outside of which the respondents demonstrated was temporarily housing the refugee claimants who were awaiting the outcome of their claims; (2) some of the participants were seen giving the *Sieg Heil* Nazi salute; (3) Nazi and American Confederate flags were used in the demonstration; and (4) the chant "White Power" was heard during the demonstration. A new trial was ordered for the accused. While the outcome at the Supreme Court of Canada is both a relief and just, the circuitous and uncertain path that the case took is inherent in the legal process. Indeed, the outcome could have been very different.

Perhaps the more common route when dealing with hate crimes within the criminal courts is that of relying on the enhanced sentencing provisions included in section 718.2 of the *Criminal Code*. (See Box 6.3) This section outlines general principles to be considered by a judge upon conviction for all offences. Certain characteristics or facts of a case are seen as "aggravating," such as the offender's use of extreme violence or considerable criminal history. In these cases, the judge might hand down

Box 6.3: Purpose and Principles of Sentencing

Purpose

718. The fundamental purpose of sentencing is to contribute, along with crime prevention initiatives, to respect for the law and the maintenance of a just, peaceful and safe society by imposing just sanctions that have one or more of the following objectives:

- (a) to denounce unlawful conduct;
- (b) to deter the offender and other persons from committing offences;
- (c) to separate offenders from society, where necessary;
- (d) to assist in rehabilitating offenders;
- (e) to provide reparations for harm done to victims or to the community; and
- (f) to promote a sense of responsibility in offenders, and acknowledgment of the harm done to victims and to the community.

R.S., 1985, c. C-46, s. 718; R.S., 1985, c. 27 (1st Supp.), s. 155; 1995, c. 22, s. 6.

Fundamental principle

718.1 A sentence must be proportionate to the gravity of the offence and the degree of responsibility of the offender.

R.S., 1985, c. 27 (1st Supp.), s. 156; 1995, c. 22, s. 6.

Other sentencing principles

18.2 A court that imposes a sentence shall also take into consideration the following principles:

- (a) a sentence should be increased or reduced to account for any relevant aggravating or mitigating circumstances relating to the offence or the offender, and, without limiting the generality of the foregoing,
    - (i) evidence that the offence was motivated by bias, prejudice or hate based on race, national or ethnic origin, language, colour, religion, sex, age, mental or physical disability, sexual orientation, or any other similar factor,
    - (ii) evidence that the offender, in committing the offence, abused the offender's spouse or common-law partner or child,
    - (iii) evidence that the offender, in committing the offence, abused a position of trust or authority in relation to the victim,
    - (iv) evidence that the offence was committed for the benefit of, at the direction of or in association with a criminal organization, or

> (v) evidence that the offence was a terrorism offence shall be deemed to be aggravating circumstances;
>
> (b) a sentence should be similar to sentences imposed on similar offenders for similar offences committed in similar circumstances;
>
> (c) where consecutive sentences are imposed, the combined sentence should not be unduly long or harsh;
>
> (d) an offender should not be deprived of liberty, if less restrictive sanctions may be appropriate in the circumstances; and
>
> (e) all available sanctions other than imprisonment that are reasonable in the circumstances should be considered for all offenders, with particular attention to the circumstances of aboriginal offenders.
>
> 1995, c. 22, s. 6; 1997, c. 23, s. 17; 2000, c. 12, s. 95; 2001, c. 32, s. 44(F), c. 41, s. 20, 2005, C.32, S. 25.
>
> Source: *Criminal Code of Canada*, RS, 1985, c. C-46.

a harsher sentence than he or she otherwise would. In other cases, there might be factors that could be considered "mitigating," such as if the offender has no criminal record or shows evidence of remorse. In these cases, the judge might sentence more leniently. Of particular relevance here is that subsection (a)(ii) specifically refers to crimes motivated by "bias, prejudice or hate, based on race, national or ethnic original, language, colour, religion, sex, age, mental or physical disability, sexual orientation, or any other similar factor" and identifies this as an aggravating factor in deciding on an appropriate sentence. Clearly, then, when a judge is satisfied that the criteria have been met, a harsher penalty should be handed down than if the crime were "not motivated by bias, prejudice or hate."

Nevertheless, some "mitigating" factors, such as the lack of a criminal record, might dilute the penalty, inject uncertainty into the sentencing phase, and perhaps weaken the extent to which this section can be relied on to respond to hate in a clear and decisive way. In addition, assessing the motives of an accused can be tricky. Does the perpetrator need to say something explicitly negative or can the social context, like the location of the crime, suffice? Can we judge the motivation of the accused from the victim's perspective? Do the actions need to be completely or only partly motivated by hate? What if the "victim" is *mistakenly* targeted as a member of a designated group?

These limitations notwithstanding, there are deeper, structural problems associated with responding to unwanted or offensive behaviour by using the criminal law, which are particularly problematic in the context of hate crimes. First and foremost, use of the criminal law forces us to respond to *individual* accounts and experiences of victimization when in fact hate is not about individuals (Perry, 2001; Roberts, 1995).

> [Hate crimes] are less about any one victim than about the cultural group they represent. Hate crime is, in fact, an assault against all members of stigmatized and marginalized communities.... It does not occur in a social or cultural vacuum; rather, it is a socially situated, dynamic process, involving context and actors, structure, and agency. (Perry, 2001, p. 1)

In addition, there are limitations reflected in the language of the criminal law that may be better reflected in terms such as "hate-motivated activity" (Jeffery, 1998). In the context of the gay and lesbian community, Faulkner (1997) prefers "anti-gay/lesbian violence" because the breadth of the former term extends beyond *Criminal Code* definitions to include harassment and actions that may not meet the high criminal standard but that constitute other forms of discrimination. The League for Human Rights of B'nai Brith Canada (2005) uses the term "anti-Semitic incidents" when referring to hate crimes against the Jewish community, which includes non-criminal forms of attacks, such as racial slurs. Indeed, while there is social significance in criminal terminology—that is, labelling something as a "crime"—this is often an inadequate and unsatisfactory route. As Perry (2001) notes,

> [t]here is widespread consensus that legalistic definitions of the concept are acceptable and adequate. Thus, the common usage of the term assumes the commission of a criminal offense, a violation of an existing criminal code ... it fails to encompass grievous violations which may nonetheless be legal (for example, the Holocaust). Moreover, legalistic definitions minimize the oppressive nature and intent of bias-motivated attacks. (p. 3)

Jeffery (1998) also notes this approach "tends to confine thinking about remedies to penal sanctions" (p. 2) when there is a range of effective responses outside the formal court processes, such as consumer boycotts, letters to newspapers, or alternative dispute resolution in place of "the slow, expensive apparatus of the formal court process that, when pressed, often churns out solutions which dissatisfy all parties concerned" (Jeffery, 1998, p. 2). Indeed, a more appropriate route for some "offences," such as denying someone a job because of his or her religion, giving students lower scores because of their ethnicity, or harassing someone in the workplace because he or she is gay or lesbian, may be through human rights codes and other bodies outside the criminal arena (Snider, 1994).

Measuring Hate

The measurement of hate crimes or hate-motivated activity in Canada reflects the full range of methods and tools used to measure other forms of victimization. Both criminal and non-criminal forms of hate-motivated activity are measured with varying degrees of accuracy by these methods. While the strengths and weaknesses of the main tools remain (as outlined in Chapter 3), there are additional considerations that emerge when measuring hate victimization.

Janhevich (2001) has shown that police services have responded to hate crimes in a variety of ways, including the implementation of policies, procedures, and the establishment of liaisons with targeted groups or hate-crimes units. For example, the Toronto Police Service has established a specialized hate-crimes unit, in addition to training of roughly 2,500 officers to "enhance the ability of Service members to recognize and respond to hate/bias activity" (Toronto Police Service, 2003, p. 1). Nevertheless, there is inconsistency in the responses of police services to hate crimes across the country (Silver et al., 2004). The League for Human Rights of B'nai Brith Canada (2005) suggests that police may not record some instances as hate crimes (e.g., painting swastikas on homes or organizations, or destroying headstones in Jewish cemeteries) because they are so frequent. In addition, victims of this type of crime may be particularly hesitant to self-identify as targets of a hate-motivated crime, especially in a fairly public forum. They may be unwilling to self-identify as a member of a minority or targeted group (such as being gay or lesbian), or may be unwilling to report a victimization as a hate crime for other, personal reasons. Indeed, Perry

(2001) argues that hate crimes are more underreported than others either because of shame/fear or because of distrust of police. This will likely result in significant underreporting and underestimation of the extent of hate crimes in a given community.

A perhaps more fundamental limitation is that police-generated data cannot assess more systemic forms of bias, such as those experienced by Aboriginal peoples, outlined above. This is exacerbated by the exclusion of activities of the state and its agencies, including the police, as perpetrators of violence. Nevertheless, Perry (2001) maintains that police-reported data, while limited, have some uses: "While inaccurate in absolute numbers, the data nonetheless may be useful as a source of information on general trends and patterns" (p. 13)

Some of limitations of victimization surveys are particularly salient due to the nature of expressions of hate. For example, victimization surveys generally exclude offences against institutions, such as mosques, synagogues, and other community agencies that might be heightened targets for hate-motivated activities. In addition, however, such surveys (along with police-reported data) make what is often a false distinction between victims and non-victims (Meirs, 1989; Stanko, 1985). This is particularly problematic for a deeper understanding of the nature of hate: as Perry (2001) has pointed out, the individual victim is really the symbol of the "other" as the target of hate, although most of the "other" category will remain non-victims as measured by such surveys.

There are many community-based organizations and agencies that have taken on the recording and reporting of hate-motivated incidents. One such example is the League for Human Rights of B'nai Brith Canada (League for Human Rights of B'nai Brith Canada, 2005), an organization whose mandate includes the elimination of racial discrimination and bigotry. B'nai Brith collects data on hate crimes across Canada, and often lobbies local police and governments for action on human rights and related issues. According to Janhevich (2001), the data collected by B'nai Brith may provide the strongest available data on anti-Semitic incidents in Canada in the last 18 years due to the consistency in the definitions used and the recording of incidents.

One distinct advantage of the agency's independence from the police is that it is free to define "hate" more broadly than strict criminal definitions. Also, because the organization has a specific focus, it can concentrate on a particular type of hate crime (i.e., anti-Semitism), and it can draw on a variety of sources to include an analysis and discussion of the impact of such incidents on individual victims and on the broader community, including victims of other forms of hate. They also have an extensive outreach and public education mandate, and are more closely connected to community sources to encourage reporting of incidents. In spite of this, Janhevich (2001) maintains that hate-motivated activity is still likely underreported and underestimated by B'nai Brith data.

Clearly, then, while we have tools to measure victimization, they are not always adequate, particularly for measuring hate and other systemic forms of victimization. "Ideally, hate crime data collection would be a continuous process that relies on multiple data sources, such as official reports, victimization surveys and ethnographic investigation" (Green et al., 2003, p. 43).

QUESTIONS FOR FURTHER CONSIDERATION

1. Can you think of other social groups (besides Aboriginal peoples) who experience systemic victimization? What data would you want to have in order to better understand the nature of their victimization and how best to respond?
2. If the criminal law is limited in how effectively it can respond to hate crimes, what alternatives do you think might help reduce the spread of hate? Can you think of ones that are *outside* the criminal process?

CHAPTER 7

Everywhere and Nowhere:
Contemporary Victims Policy in Canada

WE TURN NOW to a consideration of the contemporary context of victims in Canada. Our interest is primarily in the nature of the responses to victim issues as identified in the preceding chapters. In particular, the focus is on the extent to which policies and initiatives can have an impact on the experiences of crime victims in more than a superficial way. As will be seen, there is no shortage of activity on the victim front at local, provincial, and federal levels. However, it is not clear that, taken together, decades of victims' advocacy, negotiation, and politicization have challenged essential notions of victimhood in Canada. Mainstream approaches, which adopt a fairly narrow definition of victimization and which prioritize the criminal process as the primary site for reform, characterize most initiatives across the country. Regrettably, there is little progress in addressing the more critical and fundamental barriers to improving the social response to victims.

PROGRAMS FOR VICTIMS IN CANADA

In a manner that reflects the range of influences on the contemporary victims movement in Canada, the criminal justice system has been the focus of the majority of new or strengthened victim policies. These extend from the very early stages in the process through to the correctional stage. Kong (2004) reports that for the year ending March 31, 2003, there were at least 606 victim service agencies and 9 criminal injuries compensation programs across the country.[1] Forty-one percent of these agencies were police-based, 19 percent were based in community agencies, 17 percent were sexual assault centres, 10 percent were court-based agencies, and 8 percent were "system-based agencies" where victims are assisted throughout their contact with the criminal justice process. Their focus is primarily on providing information about the status of the victim's case, court process, or the criminal justice system. In addition, many offer support to victims as they go through the process, such as accompanying them to court and assisting them in writing victim impact statements to present at sentencing (Kong, 2004).

In addition to specific programs and services, a major initiative in many jurisdictions is the adoption of a victims "Bill of Rights." (See Box 7.1) These are symbolic statements of principles that recognize crime victims and their integral role in the criminal justice system, and the need to treat them with dignity and respect throughout their ordeal. Such statements have been adopted by the federal government and a number of provinces.

There is some evidence that many victims receive these services positively. For example, the general need expressed by victims for more information about their case and the criminal process is an established finding in victim research (Landau, 2000; Maguire, 1982; Shapland, 1984). In the context of victim impact statements, Erez (2000) notes that victims like to have input into the process and to be "heard." "Others wanted to reduce the power imbalance they felt with the defendant, resolve the emotional aspects of the victimization, achieve emotional recovery or achieve formal closure" (p. 177), particularly in cases where the accused pleaded guilty, avoiding the presentation of evidence at the trial. Clearly, many victim programs are specifically designed with these goals in mind.

At the same time, the "success" of these programs is often equivocal. At the very least, it isn't clear how to measure it. As Erez (2000) states, "[d]espite the high hopes of victim rights advocates, and the misgivings of opponents of victim participation, the inclusion of victim input in proceedings during the 1990's has had little effect on the criminal justice system and on victims' satisfaction with it" (p. 178). In addition, Erez and Laster (1999) and Young (1993) have shown the limited effect of

Box 7.1: Canadian Statement of Basic Principles of Justice for Victims of Crime

In recognition of the United Nations Declaration of Basic Principles of Justice for Victims of Crime, Federal and Provincial Ministers Responsible for Criminal Justice agree that the following principles should guide Canadian society in promoting access to justice, fair treatment and provision of assistance for victims of crime.

1. Victims should be treated with courtesy, compassion and with respect for their dignity and privacy and should suffer the minimum of necessary inconvenience from their involvement with the criminal justice system.
2. Victims should receive, through formal and informal procedures, prompt and fair redress for the harm which they have suffered.
3. Information regarding remedies and the mechanisms to obtain them should be made available to victims.
4. Information should be made available to victims about their participation in criminal proceedings and the scheduling, progress and ultimate disposition of the proceedings.
5. Where appropriate, the view and concerns of victims should be ascertained and assistance provided throughout the criminal process.
6. Where the personal interests of the victim are affected, the views or concerns of the victim should be brought to the attention of the court, where appropriate and consistent with criminal law and procedure.
7. Measures should be taken when necessary to ensure the safety of victims and their families and to protect them from intimidation and retaliation.
8. Enhanced training should be made available to sensitize criminal justice personnel to the needs and concerns of victims and guidelines developed, where appropriate, for this purpose.
9. Victims should be informed of the availability of health and social services and other relevant assistance so that they might continue to receive the necessary medical, psychological and social assistance through existing programs and services.
10. Victims should report the crime and cooperate with the law enforcement authorities.

Source: http://www.justice.gc.ca/en/ps/voc/csbp.html

victim impact statements on the outcome of criminal trials, as well as the persistence of the criminal process to focus on the offender. With respect to statements of "rights," they have neither the status of law nor can they supersede the legal rights of the accused as guaranteed in the *Charter of Rights and Freedoms*. Fattah (n.d.) notes that:

> For reasons explained earlier many of victims' rights are more symbolic than real. They look good on paper but are rarely implemented in practice and worse still, the victims are left with no recourse against non-compliance or rights violations. Nothing can be more frustrating to the victim than the painful realization that what they felt were their legitimate and lawful rights are nothing but a series of hollow promises and empty slogans. (Fattah, n.d.)

Clearly, then, we cannot assume that the adoption of some programs or the victims' perceptions alone are sufficient measures of success (Sebba, 2001). Sebba (2001) highlights the complexity of measuring "success" more clearly:

> Is [the victim involvement] intended merely to modify the procedures themselves, so as to indicate that the victim is part of the process, or is it intended to affect the *outcome* (e.g., the conviction rate or the sentence imposed on the offender)? Further, is the test of whether "change" has been achieved to be determined by some supposedly *objective* measure, or by the perceptions of participants in the process—and if so, which—the victim or the criminal justice professionals? Again, if the victim's role has indeed been modified according to one of these criteria, should this test of success be adopted in isolation, or should it be weighed up against possible adverse effects on the rights of the *defendant*—or on his/her perception of the justice of the (new) system? Further, what weight should be attributed to perceptions of this system on the part of the general public—and to cost to the public purse? Finally, are there some fundamental principles of justice that must be adhered to irrespective of all these considerations? (p. 44, emphasis in original)

Perhaps more critical, however, is that few or none of these programs, which are expanding across the country, are designed to alter the essential role of victims in the criminal justice system in any essential way. Victims are still limited to their roles as witnesses in the criminal process. Within the framework of Canadian criminal justice, the rights of victims do not, and must not, supersede those of the accused. Few are designed to prevent criminal victimization and none alter the social conditions that permit — even sustain — victimization in its various forms. And they often reproduce the social and cultural baggage that victims and non-victims alike experience in the community. "Officials have their own norms about the legitimacy of victims as well. In general, the higher the social class, power and 'respectability' of the victim ... the more seriously his or her injuries will be taken" (Snider, 1994, p. 85). Indeed, entrenched legal concepts may be turned on their head and used against the interests of victims:

> Analogous to the concept of "reasonable man" applied to defendants, practitioners use the concept of the "normal victim" to evaluate the veracity and credibility of victim input. Victim reactions that are not perceived as typical are often viewed as exaggerated, illogical and unbelievable by all legal professionals, particularly defence attorneys. (Erez, 2000, p. 171)

Indeed, there is evidence that some of the initiatives that are intended to be the most rigorous and "pro-victim" may exacerbate the social inequality already experienced by women and racialized communities. For example, mandatory arrest and/or charging policies for spousal assault have been adopted in many jurisdictions in North America as a way to increase the number of such cases that come before the courts, to deter men from assaulting their partners[2] (Dawson and Donitzer, 2001; Landau, 2000; Ursel, 1994; Valverde et al., 1995), and to take the responsibility away from assaulted women for calling police and co-operating in the prosecution of their spouses. These policies are part and parcel of a range of initiatives, including criminal courts dedicated specifically to the processing of domestic violence cases (Ursel and Brickey, 1996), judges trained in the dynamics of domestic violence who sit in those courts, and the expansion of Victim-Witness Assistance Programs to support women and other victims through the criminal process.

While often touted as highly successful in bringing more cases of domestic violence to court (Cahn, 1992; Ursel, 1994; Ursel and Brickey, 1996), such policies have negative consequences for many victims. Snider (1994) and Chesney-Lind (2002) point to a disproportionate increase in charges against men of colour, as well as for women and girls as perpetrators of domestic violence.

> There is no reason to conclude that arresting and charging more suspects is helpful to the women involved, or even that it represents the option she would have preferred. As always, the men arrested are not a representative sample of abusers—they are the abusers with the fewest resources and the least ability to resist. (Snider, 1994, p. 87)

Removing abuse from the social and political context in which it occurs by requiring criminal law intervention in all cases will "result in gendered and racialized consequences that are very serious" (Chesney-Lind, 2002, p. 86).

Policies in which agency and discretion are presumptively removed also risk reinforcing the marginal and marginalized role of women who do report, as their fate is decided by a chain of criminal justice professionals with little tolerance for the complex personal, social, and economic reasons why assaulted women do not want their spouses charged (Currie, 1995; Landau, 2000; Martin and Mosher, 1995). Indeed, the strategy risks disempowering and patronizing women while proceeding with the prosecution in their "best interests" (MacLeod, 1995).

RESTORATIVE APPROACHES: MORE THAN JUST ANOTHER ALTERNATIVE?

The most recent trend in criminal justice policy, which has significant implications for the role and satisfaction of victims, is the expanded use of alternative justice programs. Many, such as pre- and post-charge diversion, are designed to keep mostly minor and first-time offenders out of criminal court, thus saving time and resources (Landau, 2004). At the same time, specific populations of offenders may be spared the consequences of criminal convictions. Others, such as victim–offender reconciliation programs, are designed to bring the victim and offender together in a different forum to resolve the dispute in a way that permits greater victim participation and influence than the criminal trial (Wemmers and Canuto, 2002). The ability to meet face to face humanizes both the victim and the offender, removes the highly technical and legal imperatives of the trial process, and may permit a more mutually satisfactory outcome. For the most part, the roles of the victim and the offender within the larger criminal forum are not challenged.

Restorative approaches to crime and justice have also emerged in a way that is designed to challenge some of the more restrictive and punitive principles of criminal justice, and to give victims a more integrated role in the process. In particular, restorative approaches recognize that the traditional criminal process relies heavily on punishment of offenders to "resolve" crime and "promotes a clash between [victims'] rights and those of the accused while reproducing the crime-control assumption that the criminal sanction controls crime" (Roach, 1999, p. 31). Restorative justice is designed to go beyond bringing victims and offenders together to negotiate a solution outside the courtroom. "Restorative/community justice is based on the fundamental principle that criminal behaviour injures not only the victims, but also communities and the offender and that any efforts to address and resolve the problems created by the criminal behaviour should involve all of these parties" (Griffiths, 1999, p. 280). Indeed, the context is one in which there is recognition that victims and offenders are generally from the same community; that crime has an impact on families, communities, and other members of the social network of victims *and* offenders; and that the resolutions must emerge from within a community-driven, reparative paradigm. In this context, victims are not only able to have input throughout the restorative process, they maintain a considerable amount of decision-making power as well (Wemmers and Canuto, 2002).

There are different models of restorative justice and a vast range of programs that fall within its parameters. Many, such as the Community Holistic Circle Healing Program in Hollow Water, Manitoba, occur within Aboriginal communities, where restorative justice has its contemporary roots (Griffiths, 1999). Programs may be attached to the formal criminal process and used as an alternative to courtroom proceedings post-charge or at sentencing. Others, such as Peacemakers International, integrate a range of community partners and may be designed to intervene before any criminal charges are laid in a pre-emptive yet constructive way (www.peacebuildersinternational.com/). In all truly "restorative" approaches, there is an attempt to address victimization from a more reparative, integrative, and inclusive manner.

The move toward adoption of restorative approaches to crime and victimization has been swift. For many, it has become a fairly uncontroversial and sensible response to the minor property offences and first-time offenders who constitute a large percentage of cases that fill the criminal courts. Others have applied it to a full range of offences, including corporate crimes (Braithwaite, 2003) and domestic violence (Braithwaite and Daly, 1995).

Yet, in spite of the prospects for restorative justice to contribute to the reform of the victim's role in the criminal process, significant limitations remain at a number of levels. In their zeal to find alternatives to a weak and problematic process, "restorative justice" is often used to refer to programs that occur outside the formal courtroom or that bring the victim and offender together to resolve the crime, many of which have no "restorative" dimensions and exclude the victim (e.g., Bannenberg and Rössner, 2003; Umbreit et al., 2003; Wemmers and Canuto, 2002). In addition, in a comprehensive review of victims' experiences with restorative justice programs, Wemmers and Canuto (2002) found that "there was no clear evidence that victims are more satisfied than they would be in the traditional criminal justice system" (p. 26). Indeed, victims often expressed dissatisfaction over the same issues as when their case is processed through the traditional process: "lack of information, the absence of restitution and the failure by authorities to follow up on offender compliance" (p. 26).

Others have expressed concern about the number of parties who, under these models, become "victims." As Crawford (2000) states, "[h]ow far can we stretch the label of 'victim' before it becomes redundant or emptied of any symbolic or social significance that it carries?" (p. 285). Indeed, the *actual* victim becomes only one of many in the process whose experience is considered (DeVilliers, personal communication, 2003), in addition to the offender and his or her family. This risks exacerbating the view that victims' feelings and contributions are subordinate to that of offenders.

Zellerer (1999) has pointed to the critical issues in applying restorative justice models to domestic violence to diverse cultures, and whether they may meet the needs of particular communities or of victims. Her data

suggest that Inuit feel uncomfortable participating in a process that involves community residents passing judgment in a public forum on another resident. This may hinder the ability of community residents to mediate and resolve disputes in their own communities and may increase women's vulnerability. It may mean that an entirely different approach to crime will be created or recreated from traditional times, one obviously different from the criminal justice system but perhaps also one different from our current conceptions of restorative justice. (p. 354)

Perhaps most fundamental are the concerns over the failure of restorative practices to address the inequalities that many of the participants may bring to the table in their attempts to resolve the incident. This is most clearly the case involving incidents of domestic violence against children, spouses, or elderly members of the family. In particular, Goodey (2005) points out that "the power differentials that sustain violence against women and children are in danger of resurfacing in the setting of an informal restorative meeting, particularly where families or people in relationships are involved" (p. 214).

The other side of this coin is that offenders, too, come to the table from socially and economically unequal positions, at least with respect to the administration of justice, but often also in contrast to victims. We can expect these dynamics to play themselves out in the early stages of deciding who has the opportunity to participate in arenas that are alternatives to the punitive criminal process, and to be reproduced or "restored" during that process. Finally, as Cunneen (2001) has pointed out, restorative justice does not recognize the state as a perpetrator, thereby excluding crimes by the state or systemic forms of victimization, including human rights abuses. He states that these approaches do not address "how to consider the relationship between restorative justice as a remedy for the gross violation of human rights when the offender is the state and its agents" (p. 84).

It would be ill advised to dismiss outright the valuable contribution that restorative justice might make to victims and to the resolution of crimes more generally. Clearly, it provides an alternative to criminal justice reforms, which emphasize increasing the punitive elements of the criminal process and which do not convincingly improve the lives of victims, the plight of the accused, or "justice." But it cannot be considered much more than an add-on to existing, repressive practices unless it reaches deep into the roots of the structural basis for crime *and* victimization. To date, this has not occurred. "While the potential application of restorative initiatives is wide, one has to return to fundamental questions which ask 'who' benefits — victims, offenders, communities or the State" (Goodey, 2005, p. 215).

Final Comments

We must, at this point, consider the direction that the victims movement in Canada has been taking, and question whether the efforts might be more productively and justly redirected. We have seen that, while it cannot realistically be completely avoided, the emphasis on linking improvements to the lives of victims with (generally punitive) reforms in the criminal justice system is both misguided and ill advised. As Snider (1994) notes,

> [c]riminal justice lacks transformative potential because it does not operate in the same way as other mainstream institutions; it fills different ideological and structural roles. Criminal justice refers to a set of institutions whose primary role is to further social control, a task made easier if its "clients" are de-legitimized, rendered voiceless and powerless, ideologically and structurally isolated from the working class. (p. 82)

Indeed, other social and political arenas, such as the home, schools, and communities, must be more central sites for reform (Comack and Balfour, 2004; Snider, 1994) as it is here where victimization, criminalization, and the conditions that create and sustain them are most powerful. We have seen, through the data presented above, that victims, both men and women, rely most heavily on informal and formal social supports in the community, while the criminal process is, overall, rarely invoked. The irony of focusing so heavily on efforts to reform *that* process becomes hard to ignore.

At the same time, we need to be more mindful of the often exclusionary implications of how many approach "gender" and its intersection with other forms of social inequality. Again, the data give us clear direction to consider masculinity in its various forms as contributing to both victimhood and offending. Young males constitute a significant portion of victims, and men in general are grossly overrepresented as perpetrators in most crimes. The conclusion that some of the same conditions that perpetuate the vulnerability of women and girls are also at play is inescapable. Yet male vulnerability, as discussed in Chapter 2, is virtually absent from the discourses of victimhood. Including it can be done without detracting or diluting the experiences of women and girls, or without *re*-placing emphasis on men and offenders. But little progress can be made without doing so. "[T]he most urgent need is to transform the community to which abusers return, and institute structural change at this level. The chances of doing this are surely diminished when all our efforts are directed toward initiatives that end up scapegoating marginal minority males" (Snider, 1994, p. 89).

We close with words from Kim Pate, Executive Director of the Canadian Association of Elizabeth Fry Societies. Perhaps more than any other group, women in conflict with the law highlight the false distinction between "victim" and "offender," and the impact of poverty, racism, and marginalization in creating society's most vulnerable.

> In addition to challenging our own values and standards of behaviour, we must ensure that any new model of justice does not merely recreate or reinforce some of the most ingrained and systematic biases of the existing system. If we merely impose our values and expectations on others, we run the risk of imposing, albeit unintentionally or out of ignorance, further punitive approaches. (Pate, n.d.)

NOTES

1. The data include those community-based agencies that provide services to victims of crime and that receive funding from a ministry with some responsibility for justice issues. In addition, shelters for abused women and transition homes were excluded as they were included in another project. As a result, the data underestimate the number of services available to victims in the community. See Kong (2004) for details about the surveys.
2. While these policies are, for the most part, gender-neutral, they were originally implemented to address the problem of spousal violence against women. Although they are a general tool used in all spousal relationships, the vast majority of cases remain those between heterosexual couples where the male is the aggressor.

QUESTIONS FOR FURTHER CONSIDERATION

1. In reviewing the material from earlier chapters, do you think differently about victim-related issues than you did before? In what ways?
2. What are the main themes that have emerged from the discussions and the data presented throughout the text?
3. Do you see a role for the criminal justice system in addressing victims' needs? What might it be? Is there also a role for other social systems? Try to be specific in identifying how these systems might contribute to addressing and reducing victimization in society.

Selected Internet Resources

Aboriginal Legal Services of Toronto: www.aboriginallegal.ca/
African Canadian Legal Clinic: www.aclc.net/
Bell Canada Child Welfare Research Unit: www.canadachildwelfareresearch.org/
B'nai Brith Canada: www.bnaibrith.ca/
Canadian Centre for Victims of Torture: www.ccvt.org/
Canadian Human Rights Commission: www.chrc-ccdp.ca/default-en.asp
Canadian Resource Centre for Victims of Crime: www.crcvc.ca/en/
Correctional Investigator: www.oci-bec.gc.ca/
519 Anti-Violence Program: www.the519.org/programs/avp/index.shtml
International Victimology: http://www.victimology.nl/
National Clearinghouse on Family Violence: www.phac-aspc.gc.ca/ncfv-cnivf/familyviolence/
National Office for Victims: www.justice.gc.ca/en/news/fs/2005/doc_31662.html
National Organization for Victim Assistance: www.trynova.org/
Office for Victims of Crime (Ontario): www.attorneygeneral.jus.gov.on.ca/english/about/vw/ovc.asp
Office for Victims of Crime (U.S.): www.ojp.usdoj.gov/ovc/
Ombudsman Ontario: www.ombudsman.on.ca/
Ontario Civilian Commission on Police Services: www.occps.ca/
Policy Centre for Victim Issues: www.justice.gc.ca/en/ps/voc/index.html
RCMP Public Complaints Commission: www.cpc-cpp.gc.ca/
Shelternet: www.shelternet.ca/splashPage.htm
World Society of Victimology: www.world-society-victimology.de/wsv/index.aspx

References

Aboriginal Justice Inquiry of Manitoba. 1991. *Report*. Winnipeg: The Queen's Printer.

Adlaf, Edward, and Angela Paglia. 2003. *Drug Use among Ontario Students, 1977–2003: OSDUS Highlights*. Toronto: Centre for Addiction and Mental Health.

Arbour, Madam Justice. 1996. *Commission of Inquiry into Certain Events at the Prison for Women in Kingston*. Report. Ottawa: Public Works and Government Services.

Au Coin, Kathy. 2003. "Family Violence against Older Adults." In Holly Johnson and Kathy Au Coin, eds., *Family Violence in Canada, 2003*, 21–32. Ottawa: Minister of Industry, Statistics Canada, Canadian Centre for Justice Statistics.

_____. 2005a. "Family Violence against Older Adults." In Kathy Au Coin, ed., *Family Violence in Canada: A Statistical Profile 2005*, 78–84. Ottawa: Minister of Industry, Statistics Canada, Canadian Centre for Justice Statistics.

_____, ed. 2005b. *Family Violence in Canada: A Statistical Profile 2005*. Ottawa: Minister of Industry, Statistics Canada, Canadian Centre for Justice Statistics.

Bannenberg, Britta, and Dieter Rössner. 2003. "New Developments in Restorative Justice to Handle Family Violence." In Elmar Weitekamp and Hans-Jurgen Kerner, eds., *Restorative Justice in Context: International Practice and Directions*, 51–79. Devon and Portland: Willan Publishing.

Bayley, J.E. 1991. "The Concept of Victimhood." In D. Sank and D.J. Caplan, eds., *To Be a Victim: Encounters with Crime and Injustice*, 53–62. New York: Plenum Press.

Beattie, Karen. 2005. "Family Violence against Children and Youth." In Kathy Au Coin, ed., *Family Violence in Canada: A Statistical Profile 2005*, 68–77. Ottawa: Minister of Industry, Statistics Canada, Canadian Centre for Justice Statistics.

Belknap, Joanne. 2001. *The Invisible Woman: Gender, Crime, and Justice,* 2nd ed. Belmont: Wadsworth.

Besserer, Sandra, and Catherine Trainor. 2000. "Criminal Victimization in Canada, 1999." *Juristat* 20(10).

Bottoms, A.E., R.I. Mawby, and M.A. Walker. 1987. "A Localised Crime Survey in Contrasting Areas of a City." *British Journal of Criminology* 27(2): 125–154.

Braithwaite, John. 1989. *Crime, Shame, and Reintegration.* New York: Cambridge University Press.

_____. 2003. "Restorative Justice and Corporate Regulation." In Elmar Weitekamp and Hans-Jurgen Kerner, eds., *Restorative Justice in Context: International Practice and Directions,* 161–172. Devon and Portland: Willan Publishing.

Braithwaite, John, and Kathleen Daly. 1995. "Masculinities, Violence and Communication Control." In Mariana Valverde, Lynne MacLeod, and Kirsten Johnson, eds., *Wife Assault and the Canadian Criminal Justice System,* 207–235. Toronto: Centre of Criminology, University of Toronto.

Brzozowski, Jodi-Anne, ed. 2004. *Family Violence in Canada: A Statistical Profile, 2004.* Canadian Centre for Justice Statistics. Ottawa: Statistics Canada.

Brzozowski, Jodi-Anne, Andrea Taylor-Butts, and Sara Johnson. 2006. "Victimization and Offending among the Aboriginal Population in Canada." *Juristat* 26(3).

Cahn, N.R. 1992. "Innovative Approaches to the Prosecution of Domestic Violence Crimes: An Overview." In E.S. Buzawa and C.G. Buzawa, eds., *Domestic Violence: The Changing Criminal Justice Response,* 161–180. Westport: Auburn House.

Canadian Centre for Justice Statistics. 2001. *Aboriginal Peoples in Canada: Canadian Centre for Justice Statistics Profile Series.* Ottawa: Ministry of Industry, Statistics Canada, Canadian Centre for Justice Statistics.

Canadian Foundation for Children, Youth, and the Law vs. The Attorney General in Right of Canada. 2004 SCC 4.

Chesney-Lind, Meda. 2002. "Reaction Essay: Criminalizing Victimization: The Unintended Consequences of Pro-Arrest Policies for Girls and Women." *Criminology and Public Policy* 2(1): 81–90.

Chibnall, Steve. 1977. *Law and Order News.* London: Tavistock.

Christie, Nils. 1977. "Conflicts and Property." *British Journal of Criminology* 17(1): 1–15.

_____. 1986. "The Ideal Victim." In E. Fattah, ed., *From Crime Policy to Victim Policy: Reorienting the Justice System,* 17–30. London: MacMillan Press.

Clark, Lorenne, and Debra Lewis. 1977. *Rape: The Price of Coercive Sexuality.* Toronto: The Women's Press.

Cohn, Martin. 1982. "Payoff to Olson a 'Bargain,' Expert Says." *Toronto Star* (January 17): A8.

Comack, Elizabeth. 2006. "Coping, Resisting, and Surviving: Connecting Women's Law Violations to Their History of Abuse." In Leanne Fiftal Alarid and Pal Cromwell, eds., *In Her Own Words: Women Offenders' Views on Crime and Victimization*, 33–44. Los Angeles: Roxbury Publishing Company.

Comack, Elizabeth, and Gillian Balfour. 2004. *The Power to Criminalize: Violence, Inequality and the Law*. Black Point: Fernwood.

Cook, Tim. 2005. "Former Native Leader Guilty of Hate Crime: Ahenakew Lashes out at Jew, Courts: Faces Removal from Order of Canada." *Toronto Star* (July 9): A20.

Coroner's Office. 1998. Jury's Verdict and Recommendations. Inquest into the Deaths of Arlene May and Randy Iles, Toronto.

Crawford, Andrew. 2000. "Salient Themes toward a Victim Perspective and the Limitations of Restorative Justice: Some Concluding Comments." In Adam Crawford and Jo Goodey, eds., *Integrating a Victim Perspective within Criminal Justice: International Debates*, 285–310. Dartmouth: Ashgate.

Crawford, Trish. 2005. "Wounds Run Deep on Remote Reserves, Kashechewan Tip of Iceberg: Ailments Point to Larger Social Ills." *Toronto Star* (November 4): D01.

Cunneen, Chris. 2001. "Reparations and Restorative Justice: Responding to the Gross Violations of Human Rights." In Heather Strang and John Braithwaite, eds., *Restorative Justice and Civil Society*, 83–98. Cambridge: Cambridge University Press.

Currie, Janet. 1995. *Ethnocultural, Minority Women, Spousal Assault and Barriers to Accessing and Problems in Using the Justice System: A Review of the Literature*. Ottawa: Department of Justice, Canada, Research, Statistics and Evaluation Directorate.

Dawson, Myrna, and Ronit Donitzer. 2001. "Victim Cooperation and the Prosecution of Domestic Violence in a Specialized Court." *Justice Quarterly* 18(3): 593–622.

DeKeseredy, Walter W., and Brian D. MacLean. 1991. "Exploring the Gender, Race, Class Dimensions of Victimization: A Leftist Critique of the Canadian Urban Victimization Survey." *International Journal of Offender Therapy and Comparative Criminology* 35: 143–161.

DeKeseredy, Walter S., and Martin D. Schwartz. 1998. *Woman Abuse on Campus: Results from the Canadian National Survey*. London, New Delhi, and Thousand Oaks: Sage Publications.

_____, and _____. 2003. "Backlash and Whiplash: A Critique of Statistic Canada's 1999 General Social Survey on Victimization." *Online Journal of Justice Studies* 1(1).

DeVilliers, Priscilla. 2003. Untitled paper presented at "Returning the Justice to Criminal Justice," Ryerson University, Toronto, November 17.

Elias, Robert. 1986. *The Politics of Victimization: Victims, Victimology, and Human Rights.* New York: Oxford University Press.

Erez, Edna. 2000. "Integrating a Victim Perspective in Criminal Justice through Victim Impact Statements." In Adam Crawford and Jo Goodey, eds., *Integrating a Victim Perspective within Criminal Justice*, 165–184. Dartmouth: Ashgate.

Erez, Edna, and Kathy Laster. 1999. "Neutralizing Victim Reform: Legal Professionals' Perspectives on Victims and Impact Statements." *Crime and Delinquency* 45(4): 530–553.

Ericson, Richard V. 1989. "Patrolling the Fact: Secrecy and Publicity in Police Work." *British Journal of Sociology* 40: 205–226.

Ericson, Richard V., and Patricia Baranek. 1982. *The Ordering of Justice: A Study of Accused Persons as Dependents in the Criminal Process.* Toronto: University of Toronto Press.

Fattah, Ezzat. n.d. "Victims' Rights: Past, Present and Future." www.enm.justice.fr/centre_de_ressources/dossiers_reflexions/oeuvre_justice/victims_rights2.htm. Retrieved from the World Wide Web on January 13, 2006.

_____. 1986. "On Some Visible and Hidden Dangers of the Victims Movement." In Ezzat Fattah, ed., *From Crime Policy to Victim Policy – Reorienting the Justice System*, 1–14. London: Macmillan.

_____. 1991. *Understanding Criminal Victimization.* Scarborough: Prentice-Hall Canada.

_____. 1992a. "The Need for a Critical Victimology." In Ezzat A. Fattah, ed., *Towards a Critical Victimology*, 14–23. New York: St. Martin's Press.

_____. 1992b. "Victims and Victimology: The Facts and the Rhetoric." In Ezzat A. Fattah, ed., *Towards a Critical Victimology*, 29–56. New York: St. Martin's Press.

Faulkner, Ellen. 1997. *Anti-Gay/Lesbian Violence in Toronto: The Impact on Individuals and Communities.* Ottawa: Research and Statistics Branch, Department of Justice, Canada.

_____. 2002. "Research Notes: Hate Crime in Canada: An Overview of Issues and Data Sources." Under review with the *International Journal of Comparative Criminology.*

Finn, Anne, Shelley Trevethan, Gisele Carriere, and Melanie Kowalski. 1999. "Female Inmates, Aboriginal Inmates, and Inmates Serving Life Sentences: A One Day Snapshot." *Juristat* 19(5).

Fitzgerald, Robin. 1999. *Family Violence in Canada: A Statistical Profile, 1999.* Ottawa: Statistics Canada, Canadian Centre for Justice Statistics.

Friedrichs, David O. 1983. "Victimology: A Consideration of the Radical Critique." *Crime and Delinquency* 29: 283–294.

Gabor, Thomas. 1994. *Everybody Does It! Crime by the Public.* Toronto: University of Toronto Press.

Gannon, Maire. 2005. *General Social Survey on Victimization, Cycle 18: An Overview of Findings 2004.* Ottawa: Minister of Industry, Statistics Canada Social and Aboriginal Division.

Gannon, Maire, and Karen Mihorean. 2005. "Criminal Victimization in Canada, 2005." *Juristat* 25(7).

Goodey, Jo. 1997. "Boys Don't Cry: Masculinities, Fear of Crime and Fearlessness." *British Journal of Criminology* 37(3): 401–418.

_____. 2005. *Victims and Victimology: Research, Policy, and Practice.* London: Pearson Longman.

Green, Donald P., Laurence H. McFalls, and Jennifer K. Smith. 2003. "Hate Crime: An Emergent Research Agenda." In Barbara Perry, ed., *Hate and Bias Crime*, 27–49. New York: Routledge.

Griffiths, Curt Taylor. 1999. "The Victims of Crime and Restorative Justice: The Canadian Experience." *International Review of Victimology* 6: 279–294.

Hagan, Frank E. 2000. *Research Methods in Criminal Justice and Criminology*, 5th ed. Toronto: Allyn and Bacon.

Harding, Katherine. 2005. "Ahenakiw Unapologetic after Conviction, Blames Racist Judicial System, Media, Jews for Ruling He Willfully Promoted Hatred." *Globe and Mail* (July 9): A13.

Hough, Mike, and Pat Mayhew. 1983. *The British Crime Survey: First Report.* Home Office Research Study no. 76. London: HMSO.

Ismaili, Karim. 1997. "The Origins of Victim Policy in Canada." Unpublished manuscript presented at the annual meeting of the Academy of Criminal Justice Sciences, Louisville, March.

Jacobs, Beverley. 1998. *Rekindled Spirit. Research Project in Preparation for the Law Commission of Canada.* Ohsweken: Bear Clan Consulting.

Jane Doe v. Board of Commissioners of Police for the Municipality of Metropolitan Toronto et al. 39 O.R. (3d) 487.

Janhevich, Derek E. 2001. *Hate Crime in Canada: An Overview of Issues and Data Sources.* Ottawa: Statistics Canada.

Jeffery, Bill. 1998. *Standing up to Hate: Legal Remedies Available to Victims of Hate-Motivated Activity – A Reference Manual for Advocates.* Ottawa: Citizens' Participation and Multiculturalism, Department of Canadian Heritage.

Johnson, Holly. 1998. "Rethinking Survey Research on Violence against Women." In Rebecca Dobash and Russell Dobash, eds., *Rethinking Violence against Women*, 23–51. London: Sage.

Johnson, Sara. 2004. "Adult Correctional Services in Canada." *Juristat* 24(10).

Karmen, Andrew. 2001. *Crime Victims: An Introduction to Victimology*, 4th ed. Toronto: Nelson.

Kauzlarich, David, Rick A. Matthews, and William J. Miller. 2001. "Toward a Victimology of State Crime." *Critical Victimology* 10: 173–194.

Kennedy, Leslie W., and Vincent F. Sacco. 1998. *Crime Victims in Context*. Los Angeles: Roxbury.

Kong, Rebecca. 2004. "Victim Services in Canada, 2002/02." *Juristat* 24(11).

Landau, Tammy C. 2000. "Women's Experiences with Mandatory Charging for Wife Assault in Ontario, Canada: A Case against the Prosecution." *International Review of Victimology*, Special Issue on Domestic Violence 7(1, 2, 3): 141–157.

_____. 2004. "How to Put the Community in Community-Based Justice: Some Views of Participants in Post-Charge Diversion." *Howard Journal of Criminal Justice* 42(2): 131–148.

_____. 2005. "Policing the Punishment: Charging Practices under Canada's Corporal Punishment Laws." *International Review of Victimology* 12: 121–138.

Law Commission of Canada. 2000. *Institutional Child Abuse — Restoring Dignity. Responding to Child Abuse in Canadian Institutions*. Ottawa: Law Commission of Canada.

League for Human Rights of B'nai Brith Canada. 2005. *Audit of Antisemitic Incidents: Patterns of Prejudice in Canada*. Toronto: League for Human Rights of B'nai Brith.

MacLeod, Lynne. 1995. Policy Decisions and Prosecutorial Dilemmas: The Unanticipated Consequences of Good Intentions. In Mariana Valverde, Lynne MacLeod, and Kirsten Johnson, eds., *Wife Assault and the Canadian Criminal Justice System*, 47–61. Toronto: Centre of Criminology, University of Toronto.

Macmillan, Harriet, Yvonne Racine, Nico Trocmé, and Christine Walsh. 1996. *Investigation of the Measurement of Child Maltreatment by the National Longitudinal Study of Children*. Ottawa: Human Resources Development Canada.

McGillivray, Anne. 2000. *Black Eyes All of the Time*. Toronto: University of Toronto Press.

McShane, Marilyn D., and Frank P. Williams III. 1992. "Radical Victimology: A Critique of the Concept of Victim in Traditional Victimology." *Crime and Delinquency* 38(2): 258–271.

Maguire, Mike. 1982. *Burglary in a Dwelling: The Offence, the Offender, and the Victim*. London: Heinemann.

Martin, Dianne L., and Janet E. Mosher. 1995. "Unkept Promises: Experiences of Immigrant Women with the Neo-Criminalization of Wife Abuse." *Canadian Journal of Women and the Law* 8(3): 3–44.

Meadows, Robert J. 1998. *Understanding Violence and Victimization*. Upper Saddle River: Prentice-Hall.

Meirs, David. 1989. "Positivist Victimology: A Critique." *International Review of Victimology* 1: 3–22.

Mihorean, Karen. 2005a. *General Social Survey on Victimization, Cycle 18: An Overview of Findings*. Ottawa: Minister of Industry, Statistics Canada, Social and Aboriginal Statistics Division.

Mihorean, Karen. 2005b. "Trends in Self-Reported Spousal Violence." In Kathy Au Coin, ed., *Family Violence in Canada: A Statistical Profile 2005*, 13–32. Ottawa: Minister of Industry, Statistics Canada, Canadian Centre for Justice Statistics.

Ministry of Community Safety and Correctional Services. 2003. "Ontario to Require Reporting of Gunshot Wounds." Toronto: Queen's Printer. http://ogov. newswire.ca/ontario/GPOE/2004/06/23/c7677.html?lmatch=&lang=_ e.html. Retrieved from the World Wide Web on January 18, 2006.

Monture-Angus, Patricia. 1999. "Standing against Canadian Law: Naming Omissions of Race, Culture and Gender." In Elizabeth Comack, eds., *Locating Law: Race/Class/Gender Connections*, 76–97. Halifax: Fernwood.

Morrison, Allison, and Gabrielle Maxwell. 2000. "The Practice of Family Group Conferences in New Zealand: Assessing the Place, Potential and Pitfalls of Restorative Justice." In Adam Crawford and Jo Goodey, eds., *Integrating a Victim Perspective within Criminal Justice*, 207–225. Dartmouth: Ashgate.

Newburn, Tim, and Elizabeth A. Stanko. 1994. "When Men Are Victims: The Failure of Victimology." In Tim Newburn and Elizabeth A. Stanko, eds., *Just Boys Doing Business: Men, Masculinities and Crime*, 153–165. London: Routledge.

Ogrodnik, Lucie, and Cathy Trainor. 1997. *An Overview of the Differences between Police-Reported and Victim-Reported Crime, 1997*. Canadian Centre for Justice Statistics. Ottawa: Minister of Industry.

Pate, Kim. n.d. Response: "This Woman's Perspective on Justice: Restorative? Retributive? How about Redistributive?" www.elizabethfry.ca/perspect. htm. Retrieved from the World Wide Web on January 13, 2006.

Perry, Barbara. 2001. *In the Name of Hate: Understanding Hate Crimes*. New York: Routledge.

Porter, Miriam, and Avrum Rosensweig. 2005. "An Appeal for Privacy." *Toronto Star* (May 9): A19.

Pottie Bunge, Valerie. 2000. "Spousal Violence." In Valerie Pottie Bunge and Daisy Locke, eds., *Family Violence in Canada: A Statistical Profile, 2000*, 11–26. Ottawa: Statistics Canada, Canadian Centre for Justice Statistics.

Pottie Bunge, Valerie, and Daisy Locke, eds. 2000. *Family Violence in Canada: A Statistical Profile, 2000*. Ottawa: Statistics Canada, Canadian Centre for Justice Statistics.

Quinney, Richard. 1970. *The Social Reality of Crime*. Boston: Little, Brown.
_____. 1972. "Who Is the Victim?" *Criminology* 10: 314–323.
R. v. Krymowski ([2005] 1 S.C.R 101, 2005 SCC 7).
Rand, Michael R. 1997. "Violence-Related Injuries Treated in Hospital Emergency Departments." Washington: U.S. Department of Justice, Office of Justice Programs.
Rankin, Jim, Jennifer Quinn, Michelle Shephard, John Duncanson, and Scott Simmie. 2003. "Singled out: Star Analysis of Police Crime Data Shows Justice Is Different for Blacks and Whites." *Toronto Star* (March 5): A1.
Razack, Sherene. 2000. "Gendered Racial Violence and Spatialized Justice: The Murder of Pamela George." *Canadian Journal of Law and Society* 15(2): 91–130.
Reitano, Julie. 2004. "Youth Custody and Community Services in Canada, 2002/2003." *Juristat* 24(9). Ottawa: Canadian Centre for Justice Statistics.
Roach, Kent. 1999. *Due Process and Victims' Rights: The New Law and Politics of Criminal Justice*. Toronto: University of Toronto Press.
Roberts, Julian. 1995. *Disproportionate Harm: Hate Crime in Canada*. Ottawa: Department of Justice.
Rock, Paul. 1986. "Victims and Policy in Canada: The Emergence of the Justice for Victims of Crime Initiative." In E. Fattah, ed., *From Crime Policy to Victim Policy: Reorienting the Justice System*, 261–289. London: MacMillan Press.
_____. 1994. "Introduction." In Paul Rock, ed., *Victimology*, xii–xix. Dartmouth: Aldershot.
Royal Commission on Aboriginal Peoples. 1996. *People to People: Nation to Nation*. Ottawa: Minister of Supply and Service.
Ruck, Martin, and Scot Wortley. 2002. "Racial and Ethnic Minority High School Students' Perception of School Disciplinary Practices: A Look at Some Canadian Findings." *Journal of Youth and Adolescence* 31(3): 185–195.
Samuelson, Les, and Patricia Monture-Angus. 2002. "Aboriginal People and Social Control: The State, Law and 'Policing'." In Bernard Schissel and Carolyn Brooks, eds., *Marginality and Condemnation: An Introduction to Critical Criminology*, 157–174. Halifax: Fernwood.
Sebba, Leslie. 2001. "On the Relationship between Criminological Research and Policy: The Case of Crime Victims." *Criminal Justice: The International Journal of Policy and Practice* 1(1): 27–58.
Shapland, Joanna M. 1984. "The Victim, the Criminal Justice System, and Compensation." *British Journal of Criminology* 24: 131–149.
Shapland, Joanna, J. Wilmore, and P. Duff. 1985. *Victims in the Criminal Justice System*. Aldershot: Gower Publishing.
Silver, Warren, Karen Mihorean, and Andrea Taylor-Butts. 2004. *Hate Crime in Canada*. Ottawa: Statistics Canada, Canadian Centre for Justice Statistics.

Snider, Loreen. 1994. "Feminism, Punishment and the Potential of Empowerment." *Canadian Journal of Law and Society* 9(1): 75–104.

Snow, Kim, and Judy Finlay. 1998. *Voices from Within: Youth Speak Out.* Toronto: Office of the Child and Family Service Advocacy.

Solicitor General, Canada. 1983. *Canadian Urban Victimization Survey: Victims of Crime.* Bulletin 1. Ottawa: Solicitor General Canada.

_____. 1985. *Canadian Urban Victimization Survey: Female Victims of Crime.* Bulletin 4. Ottawa: Solicitor General Canada.

Sprott, Jane, Anthony Doob, and Jennifer Jenkins. 2001. "Problem Behaviour and Delinquency in Children and Youth." *Juristat* 21(4). Ottawa: Statistics Canada, Canadian Centre for Justice Statistics.

Stanko, Elizabeth. 1985. *Intimate Intrusions: Women's Experience of Male Violence.* London: Routledge and Kegan Paul.

_____. 1994. "Challenging the Problem of Men's Individual Violence." In Tim Newburn and Elizabeth A. Stanko, eds., *Just Boys Doing Business: Men, Masculinities and Crime,* 32–45. London: Routledge.

_____. 1995. "Gendered Criminological Policies: Femininity, Masculinity, and Violence." In Hugh D. Barlow, ed., *Crime and Public Policy: Putting Theory to Work,* 207–226. Oxford: Westview Press.

Stanko, Elizabeth A., and Kathy Hobdell. 1993. "Assault on Men: Masculinity and Male Victimization." *British Journal of Criminology* 33(3): 400–415.

Statistics Canada. 1993. *Violence against Women Survey.* Ottawa: Ministry of Industry.

Stermac, Lana, Peter Sheridan, Alison Davidson, and Sheila Dunn. 1996. "Sexual Assault of Adult Males." *Journal of Interpersonal Violence* 11(1): 52–64.

Tang, Kwong-Leung. 1998. "Rape Law Reform in Canada: The Success and Limits of Legislation." *International Journal of Offender Therapy and Comparative Criminology* 42(3): 258–270.

Taylor Gibbs, Jewelle, and Joseph R. Merighi. 1994. "Young Black Males: Marginality, Masculinity, and Criminality." In Tim Newburn and Elizabeth A. Stanko, eds., *Just Boys Doing Business: Men, Masculinities and Crime,* 64–80. London: Routledge.

Toronto Auditor General. 2004. *Auditor General's Follow-up on the October 1999 Report Entitled "Review of the Investigation of Sexual Assaults by the Toronto Police Service."* Toronto: Toronto Auditor General.

Toronto Police Service. 2003. *Annual Hate/Bias Crime Statistical Report.* Toronto: Toronto Police Service, Hate Crime Unit.

Trainor, Catherine. 2002. *Family Violence in Canada: A Statistical Profile 2002.* Ottawa: Statistics Canada, Canadian Centre for Justice Statistics.

Trocmé, Nico, Harriet MacMillan, Barbara Fallon, and Richard DeMarco. 2003. "Nature and Severity of Physical Harm Caused by Child Abuse and Neglect: Results from the Canadian Incidence Study." *Canadian Medical Association Journal* 169(9): 911–921.

Umbreit, Mark S., William Bradshaw, and Robert B. Coates. 2003. "Victims of Severe Violence in Dialogue with the Offender: Key Principles, Practices, Outcomes, and Implications." In Elmar Weitekamp and Hans-Jurgen Kerner, eds., *Restorative Justice in Context: International Practice and Directions*, 123–144. Devon and Portland: Willan Publishing.

Ursel, Jane. 1994. "Winnipeg Family Violence Court." *Juristat* 14(2).

Ursel, Jane, and Stephen Brickey. 1996. "The Potential of Legal Reform Reconsidered: An Examination of Manitoba's Zero-Tolerance Policy on Family Violence." In Thomas O'Reilly, ed., *Post-Critical Criminology*, 56–77. Scarborough: Prentice Hall.

Valverde, Mariana, Lynne MacLeod, and Kirsten Johnson, eds. 1995. *Wife Assault and the Canadian Criminal Justice System: Issues and Policies.* Toronto: Centre of Criminology, University of Toronto.

Viano, Emilio C. 1992. "The News Media and Crime Victims: The Right to Know versus the Right to Privacy." In Emilio C. Viano, ed., *Critical Issues in Victimology: International Perspectives*, 24–34. New York: Springer Publishing Co.

_____. 1996. "Stereotyping and Prejudice: Crime Victims and the Criminal Justice System." *Studies on Crime and Prevention* 5(2): 182–202.

Vold, George B., Thomas J. Bernard, and Jeffrey B. Snipes. 1998. *Theoretical Criminology*, 4th ed. New York: Oxford University Press.

Von Hentig, Hans. 1948. *The Criminal and His Victim.* New Haven: Yale University Press.

Walklate, Sandra. 1990. "Researching Victims of Crime: Critical Victimology." *Social Justice* 17(3): 25–42.

_____. 2000. "Researching Victims." In Roy D. King and Emma Wincup, eds., *Doing Research on Crime and Justice*, 183–201. Oxford: Oxford University Press.

_____. 2001. *Gender, Crime, and Criminal Justice.* Devon: Willan Publishing.

Wallace, Marnie. 2003. "Crime Statistics in Canada, 2002." *Juristat* 23(5). Ottawa: Statistics Canada, Canadian Centre for Justice Statistics.

Washington, Patricia. 1999. "Second Assault of Male Survivors of Sexual Violence." *Journal of Interpersonal Violence* 14(7): 713–730.

Weis, Kurt, and Sandra S. Borges. 1973. "Victimology and Rape: The Case of the Legitimate Victim." *Issues in Criminology* 8: 104-106.

Wemmers, Jo-Anne, and Marisa Canuto. 2002. *Victims' Experiences with, Expectations, and Perceptions of Restorative Justice: A Critical Review of the Literature*. Ottawa: Department of Justice, Research and Statistics Division, Policy Centre for Victim Issues.

Wolfgang, Marvin. 1958. *Patterns in Criminal Homicide*. New York: John Wiley.

Young, Alan. 1993. "Two Scales of Justice: A Reply." *Criminal Law Quarterly* 35: 355–375.

_____. 2001. *The Role of the Victim in the Criminal Process: A Literature Review – 1989 to 1999*. Ottawa: Department of Justice.

Young, Richard. 2000. "Integrating a Multi-Victim Perspective into Criminal Justice through Restorative Justice Conferences." In Adam Crawford and Jo Goodey, eds., *Integrating a Victim Perspective within Criminal Justice*, 227–251. Dartmouth: Ashgate.

Zellerer, Evelyn. 1999. "Restorative Justice in Indigenous Communities: Critical Issues in Confronting Violence against Women." *International Review of Victimology* 6: 345–358.

Copyright Acknowledgments

Boxes

Box 1.1: *Toronto Star*, "Outcry rages over $90, 000 to buy killer's confession," from *Toronto Star*, A1. Copyright © *Toronto Star*, January 15, 1982. Reprinted by permission of Torstar Syndication Services.

Box 1.2: Madam Justice Arbour, "2.3.4.3 What Occurred," from *Commission of Inquiry into Certain Events at the Prison for Women in Kingston*. Copyright © Public Works and Government Services, 1996. http://www.justicebehindthewalls. net/resources/arbour_report/arbour_rpt.htm. Reprinted by permission of the Minister of Public Works and Government Services Canada.

Box 1.3: Keith Lacey, "Justice system not designed to handle welfare fraud cases," from *Northern Life*. Copyright © Keith Lacey. http://dawn.thot.net/ Kimberly_Rogers/kria104.html. Reprinted by permission of Keith Lacey.

Box 2.1: Jim Coyle, "Two horrible stabbings, two different reactions," from *Toronto Star*, A4. Copyright © *Toronto Star*, Saturday, August 8, 1998. Reprinted by permission of Torstar Syndication Services.

Box 2.2: "Jane Doe v. Board of Commissioners of Police for the Municipality of Metropolitan Toronto et al.," from vol. 39, Ontario Reports, Third Edition (1997), 519.

Box 2.3: "Assault," from *Criminal Code of Canada*, R.S., 1985, CC–46.

Box 2.4: Joan Seager, "Slain teens don't sound 'ordinary,'" from Letters to the Editor, E8. Copyright © Joan Seager, April 11, 1998.

Box 3.1: General Occurrence Form, from Canadian Centre for Justice Statistics/ Statistics Canada.

Box 3.2: *Victimization, Main Survey – Questionnaire Package*, adapted from Statistics Canada, General Social Survey, Cycle 18, 2004, (Ottawa: Statistics Canada). <http://www.statcan.ca/cgi-bin/imdb/p2SV.pl?Function=getSurvey& SDDS=4504&lang=en&db=IMDB&dbg=f&adm=8&dis=2>. Reprinted by permission of Statistics Canada.

Box 3.3: Centre for Addiction and Mental Health, "Ontario Student Drug Use Survey," from *2005 Student Drug Questionnaire.* Copyright © Centre for Addiction and Mental Health, 2005. Reprinted by permission of Centre for Addiction and Mental Health.

Box 4.1: Maire Gannon and Karen Mihorean, "Methodology," adapted from the Statistics Canada publication *Juristat*, Catalogue 85–002, vol. 25, no. 7 (Ottawa: Statistics Canada, November 24, 2005),19. Reprinted by permission of Statistics Canada.

Box 6.1: Trish Crawford, "Wounds run deep on remote reserves," from *Life Writer*, D1. Copyright © *Toronto Star*, November 4, 2005. Reprinted by permission of Torstar Syndication Services.

Box 6.2: "Hate Crimes Provisions Under the Canadian Criminal Code," from *Criminal Code of Canada.*

Box 6.3: "Purpose and Principles of Sentencing," from *Criminal Code of Canada.*

Box 7.1: "Canadian Statement of Basic Principles of Justice for Victims of Crime," from Department of Justice Canada. http://www.justice.gc.ca/en/ps/voc/ csbp.html. Reprinted by permission of the Minister of Public Works and Government Services Canada, 2006.

TABLES

Table 4.1: Maire Gannon and Karen Mihorean, "Nature of Violent Victimizations, by Age." Adapted from the Statistics Canada publication *Juristat*, Catalogue 85-002, vol. 25, no. 7 (Ottawa: Statistics Canada, November 24, 2005). Reprinted by permission of Statistics Canada.

Table 5.1: Karen Mihorean, "Severity of Spousal Violence, by Gender." Adapted from the Statistics Canada publication *Family Violence in Canada: A Statistical Profile 2005*, Kathy Au Coin ed., Catalogue 85–224 (Ottawa: Statistics Canada, July 14, 2005). Reprinted by permission of Statistics Canada.

Table 5.2: Karen Mihorean, "Spousal Violence by Personal Characteristics of Victims, by Gender." Adapted from the Statistics Canada publication *Family Violence in Canada: A Statistical Profile 2005*, Kathy Au Coin ed., Catalogue 85–224 (Ottawa: Statistics Canada, July 14, 2005). Reprinted by permission of Statistics Canada.

Table 5.3: Karen Beattie, "Relationship of Victim and Accused in Physical and Sexual Assaults Against Children and Youth, by Age and Gender." Adapted from the Statistics Canada publication *Family Violence in Canada: A Statistical Profile 2005*, Kathy Au Coin ed., Catalogue 85–224 (Ottawa: Statistics Canada, July 14, 2005). Reprinted by permission of Statistics Canada.

Table 5.4: Karen Beattie, "Age of Victim and Type of Assault Against Children and Youth by Family Members." Adapted from the Statistics Canada publication *Family Violence in Canada: A Statistical Profile 2005*, Kathy Au Coin ed., Catalogue 85–224 (Ottawa: Statistics Canada, July 14, 2005). Reprinted by permission of Statistics Canada.

Table 5.5: Kathy Au Coin, "Number and Proportion of Older Adult Victims of Crime, by Sex and Relationship of Accused." Adapted from the Statistics Canada publication *Family Violence in Canada: A Statistical Profile 2005*, Kathy Au Coin ed., Catalogue 85–224 (Ottawa: Statistics Canada, July 14, 2005). Reprinted by permission of Statistics Canada.

Table 5.6: Kathy Au Coin, "Number and Proportion of Older Adult Victims, by Type of Crime and Relationship of Accused." Adapted from the Statistics Canada publication *Family Violence in Canada: A Statistical Profile 2005*, Kathy Au Coin ed., Catalogue 85–224 (Ottawa: Statistics Canada, July 14, 2005). Reprinted by permission of Statistics Canada.

FIGURES

Figure 4.1: Maire Gannon and Karen Mihorean, "Nature of Criminal Victimization." Adapted from the Statistics Canada publication *Juristat*, Catalogue 85–002, vol. 25, no. 7 (Ottawa: Statistics Canada, November 24, 2005). Reprinted by permission of Statistics Canada.

Figure 4.2: Maire Gannon and Karen Mihorean, "Nature of Violent Victimizations, by Gender." Adapted from the Statistics Canada publication *Juristat*, Catalogue 85–002, vol. 25, no. 7 (Ottawa: Statistics Canada, November 24, 2005). Reprinted by permission of Statistics Canada.

Figure 4.3: Maire Gannon and Karen Mihorean, "Rate of Violent Victimization, by Marital Status." Adapted from the Statistics Canada publication *Juristat*, Catalogue 85–002, vol. 25, no. 7 (Ottawa: Statistics Canada, November 24, 2005). Reprinted by permission of Statistics Canada.

Figure 4.4: Maire Gannon and Karen Mihorean, "Rate of Violent Victimizations Per 1,000, by Income." Adapted from the Statistics Canada publication *Juristat*, Catalogue 85-002, vol. 25, no. 7 (Ottawa: Statistics Canada, November 24, 2005). Reprinted by permission of Statistics Canada.

Figure 4.5: Maire Gannon and Karen Mihorean, "Rate of Violent Victimizations, by Main Activity." Adapted from the Statistics Canada publication *Juristat*, Catalogue 85-002, vol. 25, no. 7 (Ottawa: Statistics Canada, November 24, 2005). Reprinted by permission of Statistics Canada.

Figure 4.6: Maire Gannon and Karen Mihorean, "Violent Victimizations Reported to the Police." Adapted from the Statistics Canada publication *Juristat*, Catalogue 85–002, vol. 25, no. 7 (Ottawa: Statistics Canada, November 24, 2005). Reprinted by permission of Statistics Canada.

Figure 4.7: Maire Gannon and Karen Mihorean, "Location of Violent Victimizations." Adapted from the Statistics Canada publication *Juristat*, Catalogue 85–002, vol. 25, no. 7 (Ottawa: Statistics Canada, November 24, 2005). Reprinted by permission of Statistics Canada.

Figure 5.1: Karen Mihorean, "Most Serious Spousal Violence Experienced in the Last Five Years, by Gender." Adapted from the Statistics Canada publication *Family Violence in Canada: A Statistical Profile 2005*, Kathy Au Coin ed., Catalogue 85–224 (Ottawa: Statistics Canada, July 14, 2005). Reprinted by permission of Statistics Canada.

Figure 5.2: Karen Mihorean, "Frequency of Incidents of Spousal Violence, by Gender." Adapted from the Statistics Canada publication *Family Violence in Canada: A Statistical Profile 2005*, Kathy Au Coin ed., Catalogue 85–224 (Ottawa: Statistics Canada, July 14, 2005). Reprinted by permission of Statistics Canada.

Figure 5.3: Karen Mihorean, "Reasons for Reporting Spousal Violence to the Police, by Gender." Adapted from the Statistics Canada publication *Family Violence in Canada: A Statistical Profile 2005*, Kathy Au Coin ed., Catalogue 85–224 (Ottawa: Statistics Canada, July 14, 2005). Reprinted by permission of Statistics Canada.

Figure 5.4: Karen Mihorean, "Police Action in Reported Cases of Spousal Abuse." Adapted from the Statistics Canada publication *Family Violence in Canada: A Statistical Profile 2005*, Kathy Au Coin ed., Catalogue 85–224 (Ottawa: Statistics Canada, July 14, 2005). Reprinted by permission of Statistics Canada.

Figure 6.1: "Aboriginal and Non-Aboriginal Victims of Crime, per 1,000." Adapted from the Statistics Canada publication *Juristat*, Catalogue 85-002, vol. 26, no. 3 (Ottawa: Statistics Canada, June 6, 2006). Reprinted by permission of Statistics Canada.

Figure 6.2: "Aboriginal and Non-Aboriginal Victims of Spousal Violence." Adapted from the Statistics Canada publication *Juristat*, Catalogue 85–002, vol. 26, no. 3 (Ottawa: Statistics Canada, June 6, 2006). Reprinted by permission of Statistics Canada.